Whiteness

Whiteness

Feminist Philosophical Reflections

Edited by
Chris J. Cuomo
and
Kim Q. Hall

ROWMAN & LITTLEFIELD PUBLISHERS, INC.
Lanham • Boulder • New York • Oxford

ROWMAN & LITTLEFIELD PUBLISHERS, INC.

Published in the United States of America
by Rowman & Littlefield Publishers, Inc.
4720 Boston Way, Lanham, Maryland 20706
http://www.rowmanlittlefield.com

12 Hid's Copse Road
Cumnor Hill, Oxford OX2 9JJ, England

British Library Cataloguing in Publication Information Available

Library of Congress Cataloging-in-Publication Data
Whiteness : feminist philosophical reflections / edited by Chris J.
  Cuomo and Kim Q. Hall.
    p.   cm.
    Includes bibliographical references.
    ISBN 0-8476-9294-9 (alk. paper). — ISBN 0-8476-9295-7 (pbk. :
alk. paper)
    1. Whites—United States—Race identity. 2. Racism—United
States. 3. Feminist theory—United States. 4. United States—Race
relations. I. Cuomo, Chris J. II. Hall, Kim Q., 1965–   .
E184.A1W399 1999   ·
305.8'00973—dc21   99-15041
                                                              CIP

Printed in the United States of America

∞™ The paper used in this publication meets the minimum requirements of
American National Standard for Information Sciences—Permanence of Paper
for Printed Library Materials, ANSI/NISO Z39.48–1992.

Contents

Acknowledgments

This project would not have been possible without the support of the Midwest Society for Women in Philosophy (SWIP). The fact that this book emerged from sometimes difficult, sometimes playful, and often illuminating conversations about race and racism in Midwest SWIP is evidence of the collective character of feminist praxis. Many members of that feminist intellectual community have profoundly influenced our thinking about whiteness. This book is dedicated to the members of Midwest SWIP and especially to María Lugones, whose friendship and philosophical brilliance has made our lives more rich, and to Jackie Anderson, whose work has challenged and enlightened us.

We want to acknowledge and honor how much heart the contributors put into the process of writing these essays. We appreciate their honesty, their patience, their wit, and their philosophical acumen. We thank them for joining us in this venture and for the wonderful work they've shared with us.

We would also like to thank Maureen MacGrogan, editor at Rowman & Littlefield, for her helpful suggestions and encouragement at crucial moments in the process of completing this project; Dorothy Bradley, our production editor; and Jennifer Ruark for sparking the idea for this book. It has been a pleasure to work with such keen, attentive editors.

From Kim: Somewhere in the midst of this book project, I realized that I have known Chris Cuomo for ten years. We met as graduate students at a meeting of the Midwest Society for Women in Philosophy, and over the years I have learned so much from my conversations with her. It was wonderful to coedit this book with Chris, and I would like to thank her for her friendship, wisdom, and joy. I also want to thank Karen Schlanger for her patience and good cooking when we were surrounded by papers to edit. I thank Jeffner Allen for her friendship, for her unfailing support of my work, and for everything she has taught me. For their enthusiasm and good ideas I thank Kathryn Kirkpatrick, Rosemary Horowitz, Leon Louis, and Tina Groover. And, finally, I would like to thank Cressida Heyes for the gifts of her insight, encouragement, friendship, and love.

From Chris: More than usual, this project has been nurtured through conversations about the assumptions and practices that ground our everyday lives. I want to thank Kim Hall for being such a caring friend, such a generous and encouraging colleague, and such an astute wielder of the editorial pen. Working on this book together has been an unusual adventure, and I am pleased that we will be forever bound to each other through words on paper.

Thanks to Ted Morris for seemingly endless support and wisdom. Ted's treasured companion, my good friend Linda Weiner Morris, fell ill a year ago and died soon thereafter. Though Linda, a careful and wry observer of the workings of race, was unable to contribute to this volume as she had intended, her example and her voice are ever clear in my memory. I hope they are also present in my work.

Thanks to Marilyn Thie and Huntington Terrell, dear teachers who helped me know that philosophy ought to matter, and to Claudia Card for countless lessons in how to actually do such philosophy. For provocative conversations about whiteness, power, and the absurd realities of race, I thank Linda Martín Alcoff, Karen Collie, Pam Cavalier, Erin Brown, Angela Yesh, and all the members of the Honors Seminar on Philosophy and Race at the University of Cincinnati. Thanks to Bob Richardson and Larry Jost for their support of this project.

Thanks to Catherine Raissiguier and Kristin Naca for a night on the town and to Karen Schlanger, the light of my life, for letting me know when I've stopped making sense.

Introduction: Reflections on Whiteness

Chris J. Cuomo and Kim Q. Hall

$\mathcal{D}$uring the time we have been working on this book, an epidemic of hateful violence seems to have spread across the United States. In Jasper, Texas, James Byrd was chained to the back of a pickup truck and dragged for two and a half miles by two white men because he was Black. In addition to this loathsome murder, which occurred on June 14, 1998, on October 7, a gay University of Wyoming undergraduate named Matthew Shepard was pistol-whipped, tied to a fence, and left to die. Two weeks later Barnett Slepian, a Jewish doctor who performed abortions, was murdered by a sniper in Amherst, New York. It remains difficult (and often deadly) for Mexicans to cross the border into the United States, while many white Anglos vacation and shop easily and cheaply in Mexico. Black churches have been torched in the rural South while white officials scratch their heads and wonder whether the fires were racially motivated. While the media represent Native Americans as casino owners and Asian Americans as model minorities, affirmative action policies are eroded by courts sympathetic to those who claim to be victims of reverse discrimination. At the same time, so-called White Studies appears on the evening news and in the *New York Times* as an uncritical "celebration of whiteness."

In the face of what seems to be a hopeless situation, antiracist feminist activists and scholars must continue to promote strategies that resist current forms of domination. The need for such strategies is especially urgent when promoters of dominant oppressive ideologies appropriate the language of struggles for liberation even as they undermine and eliminate the gains of movements for social justice. This book is an expression of resistance and of our continuing belief in the power of feminist writing and activism to transform lives, institutions, and realities.

WHY WHITENESS?

In the last decade many scholars of history, sociology, literature, law, and philosophy have begun articulating and analyzing a fact that anthropologists have acknowledged for half a century and that some people have always known—that racial categories are socially constructed and contextually defined. These deconstructive and reconstructive academic strategies help undermine popular acceptance of biological and other naturalistic understandings of race. Unfortunately, they also create room for an uncritical view of racial geography that sees everyone as similarly located in relation to racial ideologies (because we're all equally socially constructed) and therefore as equally oppressed or liberated through racialized power. For instance, a recent television ad proclaimed "there are no races," in hopes of selling Internet services to imaginary consumers who wish to see themselves above or beyond racial categorization. A recent *Spin* magazine article suggests that when the white boy says, "Yo," he transgresses whiteness in the way that white people who performed in blackface supposedly "transgressed" whiteness earlier in this century (Aaron 1998).

What does it mean for white people to claim, even if only for dramatic effect, that "there are no races" or that racial privilege can be transgressed with fleeting gestures (and therefore need not be forfeited at all), especially in the face of so much racially motivated violence and the ubiquitous material givenness of race? Certainly we are not all the same with regard to race. Culture, social location, gender, and color are not washed away when we communicate on computer screen or when we create hybrid cultures that ambiguously reference race. Contemporary (white) media representations of a race-free society make it seem likely that trends toward thinking of race as a social construction are merely contemporary moves toward a new melting pot—toward a new hegemony of commonality that is really just twenty-first-century whiteness and white supremacy, in disguise.

But there is a more fruitful direction for scholarship and activism that is antiracist and that realizes the contingent, social nature of racial categorizations and perceptions of difference. Instead of understanding the conditional nature of racial boundaries as an excuse to deny the privilege and responsibility implicit in white identity, antiracist thinkers aim toward undermining racial hierarchies, along with false naturalistic conceptions of racial boundaries. The authors in this collection contribute to that project by focusing on the meanings and maintenance of whiteness.

Given the ubiquitous focus on Europeans in canonized histories of thought and "civilization," it might seem redundant to inquire about the history and meanings of whiteness. Don't we already know enough—too much—about white folks and their business? In response to white supremacy, racist histories, and a paucity of trustworthy scholarly work that takes the experiences of people of color as its starting point, it makes sense to focus on the history and meanings of racial categories that mark some people and some cultures as Other to white. It is therefore not surprising to find that most efforts to decode the meanings of race investigate racial categories that mark individuals and groups as not white.

But critical scholarship on whiteness also asks new questions of old stories. Because of its foundational role in justifying and maintaining racism and colonialism in the United States (and, now, most of the world), whiteness is uniquely located on the racial map. For whites to fail to consider whiteness as a historical, constructed, and dynamic category is to risk treating it as normal (rather than normalizing), uniform (not immeasurably variable), paradigmatic (instead of fundamental to racism), and given (rather than dutifully maintained). Scholars such as Ruth Frankenberg, David Roediger, Noel Ignatiev, and Vron Ware have begun to ask about the history of whiteness, the systems and practices that maintain it, and how it might be possible to resist racializing regimes and accompanying privilege: to resist the power of whiteness. Central to this work are questions about how it is that culture and the state create such a wide range of different folk who understand themselves as white.

Scholars and activists critically interrogating whiteness seek to decenter rather than recenter whiteness by making performances of whiteness visible. As more than phenomenology, critical scholarship on race, including whiteness, connects investigations of lived racial categories to the elimination of white supremacy. But *how* are we to discuss whiteness without once again putting it "in the center"? Naomi Zack notes in her contribution to this volume that there is something off-putting and potentially dangerous about white people discussing whiteness. When those who are white discuss their racial background and identity, their remarks often seem confessional, apologetic, or like attempts to distance themselves from racist legacies. Indeed, in compiling this book we found it difficult to eliminate the confessional trope without also cutting out important information about how whiteness and white supremacy get reproduced. Yet talking about whiteness need not keep attention on white people; one need not be an insider to a class to reveal its secrets. While some of us who are not white might find it a waste of time to contemplate and examine whiteness, it is undeniably true that some of the most important recent work on whiteness is written by people who are not white, or not so white.

Unfortunately, much discussion of whiteness in popular media has made critical scholarship on whiteness appear to be one among a variety of schools of ethnic study. The logic is often spuriously presented in the following way: since Native Americans have Native American Studies, African Americans have African American Studies, Latinas and Latinos have Latin American Studies, Asians have Asian American Studies, and women have Women's Studies, it is time for white people (white men?) to have White Studies. Such an understanding misconstrues multiculturalism as a liberal inclusion of diverse groups and renders invisible the material realities of institutionalized racism, sexism, heterosexism, and anti-Semitism that inspired the formation of women's studies, ethnic and area studies, and other resistant forms of scholarship.

By representing studies of whiteness as simply one among many tributaries in the study of culture, the popular media have made critical, antiracist, and postcolonial scholarship on whiteness appear akin to white male fears of reverse discrimination and white supremacist characterizations of whiteness as just another (neutral) ethnicity. The claim that the need to study whiteness is equivalent to the need to study black, Latina/Latino, and indigenous identities, histories, and cultures makes oppression invisible and obfuscates the extent to which most "studies" already are "white." In addition, popular discussion of the study of whiteness has ignored what is at the heart of much critical scholarship on whiteness: analyses of the relationships between the construction of whiteness and the realities of racism, and politics that hope for a connection between understanding racial formations and resisting racisms. In contributing to such scholarship, what we are after here is neither a melting pot nor an apolitical pastiche of interesting identities but a feminist, postcolonial, multicultural engagement with lived racial reality.

CRITICAL CONTEXTS

Although queries about the meanings of whiteness are becoming more prevalent, it is clear that we are still near the beginning of a long conversation about resistance to white supremacy through the reconstruction of race. New tools must be continually recrafted for the conversation to progress. This book comes out of a conversation about the meanings of whiteness that began in an intellectual and political community to which several contributors belong, the Midwest Society for Women in Philosophy (SWIP). In a typical SWIP divergence from standard academic presentation, for one meeting conference participants were asked to write personal narratives on whiteness, and each was invited to read her narrative aloud. Most of the participants were white. Some narratives described struggles to come to terms with white privilege. Some articulated rage at white racism. Some strove to make sense of experiences shaped at the crossroads of race, gender, class, and sexuality. Many voiced shame and pain.

Our responses to each others' words were as varied as the narratives themselves. Some worried that focusing on whiteness in the narratives reinforced the central place of white women in academic feminism. One African American woman said that while she thought such an exercise was important for white women, she did not particularly want to have to hear about white women's pain and shame as they confessed the racism that characterized their growing-up environments. In the end, there seemed to be a consensus that, as a political and intellectual community, we needed to continue to study and think critically together about race. Eventually, we decided to hold a weekend-long SWIP Institute on Racial Formation. The conversations at the Institute led to the creation of a panel on whiteness at the Central Division meeting of the American Philosophical Association, and our participation on that panel led to the conception of this book.

This work, like the SWIP sessions, is indebted to women of color who have created a more inclusive and radical feminism and who have called on white feminists to take responsibility for recognizing and organizing against racism. Like many others, our conception of feminism as we enter the twenty-first century has been shaped by the work of women of color. For example, the publication nearly twenty years ago of Gloria Anzaldúa and Cherríe Moraga's *This Bridge Called My Back: Writings by Radical Women of Color* made clear the hypocrisy and danger in white feminists' failure to take responsibility for racism and white privilege. "Radical women of color"—a name that marked a political, not simply racial identity—argued that as long as feminist theory ignored the fact that race and gender are intertwined and that females are differently situated in relation to structures of racial power and privilege, feminism will fall short of its goal to understand the "oppression of women." A number of white feminists accepted the invitation to work toward understanding the ways in which racial formation and racism complicate simplistic understandings of categories such as "white" and "woman." Minnie Bruce Pratt, Mab Segrest, Adrienne Rich, Marilyn Frye, and Ruth Frankenberg published work on how whiteness shapes and maintains racist and sexist regimes. Radical thinkers from various social locations began to think about how race shapes and is shaped through gender, privilege, and other aspects of identity. The models provided by *This Bridge*; *Home Girls: A Black Feminist Anthology*, edited by Barbara Smith; and the work of philosophers María Lugones and Elizabeth V. Spelman, because of their explicit reformulation of gender as always intermingled with and by race, class, and sexuality, helped generate feminist philosophies that begin with thinking from the intersections of sites of difference.

Despite the widespread, if hidden, influence of the work of radical women of color to contemporary political thought, it is appalling how little their perspectives count as authorities on race. In the 1990s—witness recent media frenzies around conflicts involving African American men—white men and African American men seem to listen and respond to each other as if the huge amount of scholarship by feminists of color (and the growing body of work by antiracist white feminists) doesn't exist. In Marlon Riggs's film *Black Is, Black Ain't*, bell hooks captures the ways in which contemporary discussions of race are discussions between white men and men of color when she says that the dominant conversation about race in academia and in the popular media is a "dick thing." In the introduction to *Killing Rage* she writes:

> When race and racism are the topic in public discourse the voices that speak are male. . . . When race politics are the issues, it is one of the rare moments when white men prick up their ears to hear what black men have to say. No one wants to interrupt those moments of homo-social patriarchal bonding to hear women speak. Given these institutionalized exclusions, it is not surprising that so few women choose to publicly "talk race." (hooks 1995, 2)

These exclusions are even more enraging when men of color and white men use feminists insights to ground their theorizing about race while ignoring the ways in which race and racism are gendered. It is perhaps only a matter of time before traditionalist male scholars announce their "discovery" of what the Combahee River Collective argued in 1978—that we must theorize the intersections of gender, race, class, and sexuality in our analyses of race.

ON NARRATIVE PHILOSOPHY

Critical race theory has illuminated the extent to which familiar tools of analysis—Marxism, positivism, critical theory, feminism—often lack central, deep interrogation of the history and social significance of the construction of race. Accordingly, some of the most important work to be done by antiracist scholars is very basic, involving critical social history as well as contemporary phenomenological reflections on the varieties of whiteness, white collusion, antiracist teaching, transgression of racial norms, and the inevitability and fluidity of the meanings of bodies.

We solicited contributions for this book by invitation and through a widely distributed call for philosophical narrative essays reflecting on meanings of whiteness in racist, sexist, heterosexist, anti-Semitic, and capitalist contexts. We tried to maintain an emphasis on narrative for a number of reasons. First, our experiences teaching classes on philosophy and race left us frustrated by the lack of accessible, critical, and multivocal work on whiteness. The use of narratives in classroom discussions about gender and racialization invites students to also use their experiences as points of departure for thinking about how the meanings of race both reinforce and resist white supremacy. We hoped that reflective narratives would make available openings for readers to explore their own knowledge and experience and also to revise and challenge the claims that are presented here. Thus, we asked contributors to write personal narratives in which they explored the politics of experience.

Putting together a collection of "philosophical narratives" has not been easy. When we were composing the call for essays, we naïvely anticipated being overwhelmed with contributions. We imagined a lively ersatz community of theorists who were dying to convey their insights and their research in a less formal, more personal voice. In fact, though the call for essays was posted far and wide, we received fewer contributions than expected. Wondering why, we considered how the call for personal narratives rather than traditional disciplinary papers might have influenced response. Personal narratives are far more risky than scholarly essays. Indeed, some of the more prominent feminist philosophers, women whose perspectives we hoped to include in the book, did not want to write narratives. After hearing our descriptions of this project and our enthusiastic invitation to contribute, one philosopher admitted that she was afraid to write a narrative because what she would say would be very painful and potentially hurtful to members of her family. Her willingness to acknowledge honestly what made writing personal narratives about race so difficult reminded us of the safety provided by the scholarly conventions of philosophical writing.

Safety is possible in theoretical prose because the theorist is able to create and maintain distance. Conventional theoretical prose can be personal in the sense that the theorist might address issues that are particularly relevant to her, or use experience or a real example to ground her theory. But generally, self-disclosure in philosophy is minimal and has little significance beyond the abstract question at hand. It is one thing to write indirectly about issues that have shaped one's experiences and to use insights gleaned from personal experience to generalize about women's lives in white supremacist heteropatriarchy. It is another matter to write in such a way that the theorist makes clear what is at stake for her personally in the discussion without hiding behind technical jargon. To the extent that narrative makes a writer vulnerable in ways that standard theoretical prose does not, it is easy to understand why many feminist theorists enjoy the safety of academic convention. In addition, it is impossible to base universal claims on a personal narrative. And what is philosophy without universal claims?

Fortunately, not all philosophical thinkers have conceived of philosophy as a matter of constructing pure categories and making abstract universal claims. Gramsci distinguished between "traditional" intellectuals who were arms of State power and organic intellectuals who maintained a critical and reflexive perspective on their place in social structures. Feminist philosophers such as Joyce Trebilcot have distinguished between philosophical methods and projects that are essentially "canon maintenance" and those philosophical methods and projects that seek to understand how they are informed by and participate in relations of power in the world. As Bettina Aptheker observes of Adrienne Rich's *Of Woman Born*, Rich does not use her own experience to make universal claims about women's experiences of child birth and mothering. Rather, in grounding her analysis of mothering on personal experience, Rich offered an innovative method for feminist theorizing, and encouraged others to do the same.

Despite the feminist cliché that the personal is political, many feminist theorists seem reluctant to include personal narratives in their theorizing. In fact, as feminist philosophy becomes increasingly institutionalized, many have come to avoid narrative in their quest for philosophical legitimacy. But what is lost from feminist theorizing in this flight from the personal? When we seek the security of the omniscient, detached scholarly voice, philosophers risk compromising personal and political honesty. At present, it seems as if much of feminist theory has lost its edge, its connection to everyday struggles and victories, and its power to encourage shifts in consciousness. While there is no guarantee that narratives convey "the truth," they do invite writer and reader to locate herself in relation to the issue at hand, to struggle along with others. In the context of feminist writings about whiteness, personal narratives provide a space in which theorists might expose our struggles with racial formation and racism. The form of narrative makes it difficult to write about whiteness and racism as if they do not affect us every day, and to convey information without exploring its emotional dimensions and impact. As Alison Bailey notes in her contribution to this book, whiteness involves ways of being in the world, performances that resemble what we think is natural only because they have been unconsciously repeated over long periods of time. If critical interrogations of whiteness involve paying attention to how whiteness is performed, then its affective dimensions cannot be dismissed. The narratives in this collection invite further reflection on whiteness as serious drama, as high comedy, as shameful, horrific, mysterious, and mundane.

There are epistemic and political dangers in using personal experiences as though their truth cannot be questioned or particularities analyzed. The worry, expressed most notably by historian Joan Scott (1991), is that interpreting experience as truth obscures the discursive construction of experience, and thus the extent to which any perspective, any narrator, exists within a nexus of political economies that are not self-evident, and not evident to the self. The pitfalls and dangers of narrative are manifold, and it is crucial to interpret and investigate experience in ways that do not misrepresent narrative, reminiscence, and testimony as given, or beyond question. Still, we have witnessed a tendency in students and people who do not work in the production of theory to take formal scholarly writing to represent truth (even when the scholarship rejects "Truth") and narratives to convey "mere opinion." We have therefore found students more likely to argue about, disagree with, contextualize and pick apart writing that is informal, colloquial, and exposed. We encourage your critical responses to the historical, social, and political realities that inform the narratives herein. We hope these essays will help you develop your own living theories about meanings of race, and your own resistance to the givens of whiteness.

THE ESSAYS

The essays in this volume sit in uncomfortable relation to legacies of uncritical reflections on whiteness. In the confessional mode that often characterizes offerings of a repentant oppressor some white writers have elsewhere represented themselves as clean, or innocent, by relaying reconstructed memories of childhood. While childhood narratives can be a helpful point of departure for attempts to understand early training or resistance to racist cultures, backward glances to the "innocence of childhood" can also serve as distractions from facing up to complicated ethicopolitical realities, including the impossibility of moral purity. Childhood narratives about racism are sometimes offered in ways that promote what María Lugones (1990) calls the *infantilization of judgment*, which involves "a dulling of the ability to read critically, and with maturity of judgment, those texts and situations in which race and ethnicity are salient." She writes, "It appears to me as a flight into a state in which one cannot be critical or responsible: a flight into those characteristics of childhood that excuse ignorance and confusion, and that appeal to authority" (52–53).

Images of white children who are as innocent and oblivious to race and racism as they are to the fact that they are not the center of the universe reinscribe notions of whiteness as normal and harmless, and as a source of purity and innocence corrupted when it comes into contact with nonwhite Others, and reinscribe responsibility for racism as always resting with someone else.

The backward-looking narratives included here disrupt and deconstruct assumptions of innocence, and interrogate early experiences of race in order to locate axes of power and complicity with racism. Linda López McAlister understands her Mexican grandmother's passing as white through reflections on her own awkward experiences as a lesbian attempting to pass as straight. With a critical, compassionate eye, she investigates her own complex identity by addressing a long-standing familial and racial mystery. For Kim Hall, the layers of whiteness are symbolized more starkly in childhood memories of a Confederate flag hanging in the basement, and in the explicit demands of southern white womanhood.

Amy Edgington evokes a slightly earlier white southern moment in memories of bus desegregation. Like Kim Hall, she describes the evolution of an actively antiracist identity. Both writers complicate stereotypes of white southern racism while refusing to deny the impact of social geography on race and gender.

Unsettling the unity of the category "white," Linda Pierce inhabits an identity that is both white and not white. Her depiction of the tensions and intersections among feminist, antiracist, and postcolonial consciousness raises crucial questions about family, politics, and the academization of activism.

The writers in Section Two look at intentional and accidental performances of whiteness, as well as attempts to disrupt what the world takes to be white. Judy Scales-Trent bears witness as an observer on the boundaries of white and black. Taken to be white by a white cab driver, she finds it possible to rhetorically reinsert herself as black, though she cannot erase the harm caused by her unchosen exposure to "insider" knowledge in a racist culture. On the flip side of racial reality, Chris Cuomo discovers, also unintentionally, that in attempting to pass as a man she runs the risk of losing white privilege.

Laurie Fuller chronicles some of her successes and failures as a white teacher seeking to complicate students' conceptions of race, gender, sexuality, and identity. She compares her experiences using the terms *whitie* and *dyke* in the classroom and encourages similar experiments with rhetorical transgressions of racial norms.

Section Three opens with a critical essay by Naomi Zack. Zack is suspicious of discussions of whiteness, and so she analyzes some of the central tropes in self-described antiracist studies of whiteness. Among the objects of her inquiry is the concept of "white privilege," which Alison Bailey also takes as a point of departure. Interestingly, Bailey finds "privilege" more useful, though she uncovers some strange logic behind the assumption that to recognize undeserved privilege is to find oneself in a dilemma.

Finally, Lisa Tessman and Bat-Ami Bar On offer a travelogue/meditation-in-two-voices on whiteness, Jewish identity, nation, and privilege. Contrasting the perspectives of an American Jew and an expatriate Israeli Jew, thinking together while traveling in Israel, their discussion highlights the relationships between hegemony and cultural lens, the tensions among different constructions of "white" and "Jew," and the limits of an American take on the global realities of race.

Though we've clustered these essays around common themes and writing styles, we hope readers will gravitate to the essays in whatever order suits their own interests. To begin with a critical edge, turn first to Zack's thoughts on "White Ideas." For a brief encounter with "The American Celebration of Whiteness," read the essay by Scales-Trent. If you are an activist, you might be most drawn to the contributions by Pierce and Edgington. In any case, we hope you find good company here as you wonder about the meanings of race, gender, sexuality, and class, and as you imagine a world without racism.

WORKS CITED

Aaron, Charles. "What the White Boy Means When He Says Yo: Coming of Age in Hip-Hop America." *Spin*, November 1998: 119–20.

Aptheker, Bettina. *Tapestries of Life: Women's Work, Women's Consciousness, and the Meaning of Daily Experience.* Amherst: University of Massachusetts Press, 1989.

Gramsci, Antonio. *Selections from the Prison Notebooks of Antonio Gramsci*, ed. Quintin Hoare and Geoffrey Nowell Smith. London: Lawrence & Wishart, 1971.

hooks, bell. *Killing Rage, Ending Racism.* New York: Holt, 1995.

Lugones, María. "Hablando Cara a Cara/Speaking Face to Face: An Exploration of Ethnocentric Racism." In *Making Face, Making Soul/Haciendo Caras: Creative and Critical Perspectives by Women of Color*, ed. Gloria Anzaldúa. San Francisco: Aunt Lute, 1990.

Joan Scott, "The Evidence of Experience." *Critical Inquiry* 17 (Summer 1991), 773–97.

Trebilcot, Joyce. *Dyke Ideas: Process, Politics, Daily Life.* Albany: State University of New York Press, 1994.

Section One

Glancing Backward

· 2 ·

My Grandmother's Passing

Linda López McAlister

*T*his is a story about how my Mexican American grandmother, María Velarde, became an Anglo woman, Mary Douglas, and what it apparently meant to her to be perceived as "white." It's also a story about me and my mother and how my grandmother's determination to be seen as an Anglo lady affected our lives as well. And it's my attempt, after years of confusion and sadness surrounding the events in the story, to come to an explanation of what happened that finally makes some sense to me. I am also writing this because I think that my grandmother's story, while perhaps an extreme case, is not at all unique among Mexican American women, at least of her and my mother's generations. By looking at the concrete reality of one woman's story, I hope I can cast some light on the significance whiteness has for other U.S. Latina women as well.

My grandmother was born María Velarde in the border town of San Elizario, Texas, in 1881. Her mother, María Melchora Velarde-López, came from Mexico and is remembered by her grandchildren as a quiet, dark-skinned woman who dressed in black and spent most of her day in the kitchen cooking for her large family. My grandmother's father, Gabriel Velarde, came from farther up the Rio Grande Valley between Santa Fe and Taos. As is the case with many descendants of the early Spanish settlers in New Mexico, he had light skin and considered himself "Spanish" rather than "Mexican." After living with his parents in rural Northern New Mexico early in their marriage, the young family settled in the El Paso area in the 1870s to work for the Santa Fe Railroad; later the Santa Fe transferred them to the little desert town of Needles, California, where the Colorado River forms the border with Arizona.

It was certainly, at least in part, Gabriel Velarde's doing that his seven daughters grew up thinking that white was beautiful and darker skin tones were not. (My mother recalls how as a little girl she was the favorite among

15

his many grandchildren. He called her *mi rubia*—"my blonde"—and she understood even as a small child that it was her fair skin, blue eyes, and chestnut brown hair that won her favorite grandchild status. This valorization of whiteness and its concomitant devaluation of dark skin was—and often still is—the prevailing view of not only the dominant Anglo culture in the Southwest but of many Mexican Americans as well.) So the attitude that my grandmother and great aunts internalized as they grew to adulthood in their Mexican American home didn't just come solely from the prejudices of their father; rather, it permeated their world. And it's no wonder that four of the seven Velarde daughters married Anglo rather than Mexican American men. In my grandmother's case, it was a young Irish American man named Homer Sherwood from upstate New York whom she married. He was unusual among these Anglo husbands in that he had come to the Southwest already fluent in Spanish and he appreciated and made efforts to fit into my grandmother's family and culture. Thanks to him their children—my mother and her siblings—grew up in Mexican American communities in California and Arizona, if not exactly immersed in Mexican American culture, at least at home in it. They spoke Spanish at home and didn't learn English until they went to school, where the nuns promptly forbade them to speak Spanish, and it was a matter of sink or swim in English. (My mother's lifelong nickname, Nina, comes from her first teacher's misunderstanding when my mother told her she was called *niña* at home.) But Homer Sherwood died in 1924 and his widow María, with two teenage daughters to care for, soon married a man named "Shorty" Douglas, an oil tool salesman from Ohio, who came west for the oil booms of the 1920s and 1930s; he had no connections to or interest in Mexican American culture. And the transformation of María Velarde Sherwood into Mary Douglas began.

Years later, when I was growing up in the 1940s and 1950s in the patchwork of segregated neighborhoods that made up southeast Los Angeles, my parents bought a home in a working-class subdivision in the shadow of the Firestone Tire and Rubber Company. Our house was on the first street on the "right side of the tracks" that run along Alameda Street and formed the line of demarcation between our white neighborhood of Firestone Park and the predominantly Black and Mexican American community of Watts. When I was about seven or eight, I learned that our subdivision was "restricted" to whites only when a Filipino physician and his family tried to buy a house there and were dissuaded from doing so when some of the residents went door to door asking their neighbors to sign a petition demanding that the restrictive covenants in their deeds be enforced. That explained why no "Negroes or Mexicans" (as they were then called) ever tried to move in.

No one ever tried, that is, except my mother, but then with her fair complexion and the Anglo-sounding name of Nina McAlister (rather than her birth name Elena María), no one ever suspected that she was anything but 100 percent Anglo. Only a few very close friends knew otherwise, and they seemed to remember it only when they wanted her chili recipe or when their kids needed help on their Spanish homework, or someone wanted something translated. But my mother, despite her light brown hair, blue eyes, and unaccented English, is Mexican American—a fact that she doesn't deny but certainly doesn't call attention to except when there is some special reason to let her heritage be known. Even so, she has not entirely avoided the sting of racism. (A notorious piece of our family lore is the time my father's brother tried—unsuccessfully, I'm happy to report—to break up my parents' budding romance by telling his mother, "Mickey's dating a Spic!") But from the time she left home at seventeen and married my father (who was an Irish American from Oklahoma with one Cherokee great-grandmother), my mother has, in effect, passed for Anglo both in the eyes of the world and, to a large extent, in her own eyes as well. In doing this she has accomplished what her mother had tried and failed to do. And this brings me to the stories I want to tell here—my grandmother's and my own.

In 1957 I graduated from high school and was getting ready to go to college. Because my mother worked as a secretary at Firestone, I was eligible to compete for a college scholarship for children of Firestone employees, which, indeed, I won. (Small recompense, I think now, for my mother's years of devoted labor and the whole family having to listen, twenty-four hours a day, to Firestone's factory noises, smell its stinky rubbery smells, and breathe the air its smokestacks were constantly fouling. But at the time it made my family and me very proud and happy, and it gave me the precious freedom to go to college wherever I wanted.) I am the only person on either side of my family who has ever gone to college, and my parents, having been relieved of the expense of paying for my college education, decided to splurge and give me the most wonderful graduation present any of us could possibly imagine—a trip to Hawaii for me, my parents, and my grandmother, accompanied by our next-door neighbors and Helen Wilkes, the teenage daughter of some close family friends.

I was particularly happy that my grandmother got to come with us on the trip. She had recently been widowed for the second time, and she was the person I loved most in the world. For as long as I can remember, one of my greatest treats was to stay at her house for a weekend or a week or, in the summer, even longer. I loved being around her as she did her daily chores, usually singing softly to herself in Spanish (and teaching me the words to her songs). I loved working with her in her garden, helping her cook, and doing the wash in the big old-fashioned wringer/washer in the garage. We often spent afternoons together pursuing another mutual interest, reading movie magazines, for she was avidly interested in the gossip about glamorous Hollywood stars (though I don't recall her actually going to movies). Best of all I liked to go with her to a little Mexican *mercado* in San Pedro where we bought freshly made *tortillas* and *ristras* of dried red chiles when we were going to make *enchiladas*—a somewhat rare occurrence since Shorty Douglas was a meat-and-potatoes man who wouldn't eat *frijoles* or *enchiladas* under any circumstances. She always had to cook separately for him when she made Mexican food for my family.

During the thirty years of her second marriage, my grandmother always called herself Mary, never María. In fact she rarely spoke Spanish at all, except for occasional habitual phrases she used with close relatives (to me: "*Ay, como friegas!*" when I got on her nerves, or "*Diga te fue bien!*" when she would give me a little gift or treat), or as euphemisms for bodily parts and functions, or when she was talking to my mother and didn't want me to understand what she was saying. I didn't notice it then, but I realize now that I never once heard her speak Spanish in public, not even when we would go to Mexico for an occasional Sunday outing. In fact, she became especially "the Anglo lady" when we went there.

One day when we were in Honolulu we hired a limousine and a driver to drive us all on a sightseeing trip to the far side of the island. My grandmother was sitting in the front seat while Helen and I were sitting together in the rear. Our conversation turned to the question of ancestry; Helen said she was a mixture of English and German, and she asked what I was. I said I was Irish and American Indian and, with a wave in my grandmother's direction I added, "Mexican."

I will never know exactly what went through my grandmother's mind and heart when she heard me say those words, but it must have caused her terrible pain because, from that moment on, she virtually never spoke to me again. At first, since she didn't say anything to me there in the car, I was oblivious to her feelings. But soon enough it became obvious that she was furious and I was the object of her fury. When my mother tried to find out what the trouble was, the source of my grandmother's anger came out. I had "called her a Mexican." To her that was such a grievous offense that she could not bring herself to let it pass or forgive me for it. All during the voyage home to California I tried, with my mother's help, to make amends. My mother understood perfectly that I had meant no offense, that I had been giving information, not hurling racial epithets, and she tried, with no success whatsoever, to convince my grandmother of it. I tried apologizing, but my apology went unheeded. Eventually it became clear that, for all intents and purposes, my grandmother had passed out of my life for good the moment those offending words came out of my mouth.

That fall I went off to New York to college, and by the time I returned to California my grandmother had had a stroke, making communication difficult. There was no sign that her anger at me had abated. In the years before she passed away, which she spent, frail and disabled, in a nursing home, she didn't speak much at all. Ironically, the few words that did pass her lips were in her mother tongue, Spanish.

As a young woman I didn't realize just how much the loss of my grandmother's esteem and love affected me. But years later, the effects of that loss can still surface in my reactions and behavior, in trivial things such as my total attachment to my grandmother's Spanish-style furniture that I inherited and not so trivial matters such as an abiding fear of abandonment. By now I have spent decades trying to understand this bewildering and abrupt passing out of my life of a person I loved so much, trying to figure out the elements that contributed to the vehemence of her reaction, and trying to find my own identity in relationship to my Mexican American heritage.

My first thought was that my grandmother had just misunderstood what was happening: she thought I was calling her a name when I was just giving information about her and my ethnic background. It's true enough that words such as "You (blankety-blank) Mexican" would have been understood by anyone as an ethnic slur. But those were not the words I used. The words I did use were uttered wholly without malice—more likely, they were tinged with pride, for the things that I liked best about my grandmother were the things that were reflections of her ethnicity. But if it had been a simple misunderstanding of this sort, it should have been easy to clear up.

Then I thought maybe she believed I was telling Helen that she was from Mexico and she was angry because she was born in Texas and had been a U.S. citizen all her life. This seemed to be a somewhat more plausible explanation because my grandmother had lived all her life close to the U.S.-Mexican border. She and her family lived in Bisbee, Arizona, practically on the border, during what she used to call "the Pancho Villa war." Frequent border incursions made it significant which side of the border you were born on. And she lived through the Depression when, in her part of the world, the U.S. government regularly rounded up "Mexicans" and unceremoniously deported them to Mexico, sometimes without bothering to find out whether they were U.S. citizens. It's interesting to note that from the time of the U.S. annexation of Mexican territories after the Mexican War, the same word, "Mexican," was used by Anglos to designate both Mexican nationals and Mexican Americans.[1] Even in 1957 we still didn't have the words "Mexican American" or "Chicana" to describe my grandmother; we were still using "Mexican" for everybody of Mexican heritage regardless of where they were born or their citizenship. We did have some less polite words, too, such as "*pachuco,*" as some of the "tough" Mexican kids at school were called (of whom there were very few in 1957 and almost all of whom were completely excluded from the white mainstream high school culture).

But I have never found either of these two "misunderstanding" explanations adequate for explaining the intensity of my grandmother's rage. Surely if it had been just a case of this kind of misunderstanding, once things were sorted out we could have had a reconciliation. Since all attempts at reconciliation failed, it seems to me that the offense to my grandmother must have gone far deeper. My next thought was that her response must have been related to her internalization of the negative stereotypes and attitudes about Mexicans that abound in the dominant white Anglo culture of Texas and the desert Southwest where she grew up. Mexicans are supposed to be lazy, slow, stupid, greasy, and dishonest; the women are supposed to be either sexy and tempestuous or reserved and pious, while the men are stereotypically macho, domineering, beer guzzling, and violent. It is, I think, a sign of the extent to which my grandmother and her sisters believed these stereotypes about themselves that so many of them married outside their ethnic group and began to move, sooner or later, away from their original culture, language, and traditions toward those of the Anglo community into which they married.

One of my great aunts, Petra, did marry a Mexican American, a man by the name of Jorge Acuña; he was a *Californio*—a descendant of a family who had lived in California before it was ceded to the United States by Mexico. He was the town marshall in Needles as early as 1905 and one of the few Mexican Americans in a position of some power and status in Needles. But this only postponed the rush to assimilation with white,

Anglo culture for one generation. Every one of Jorge and Petra Acuña's daughters married Anglos and assimilated, as best they could, into Anglo culture. By the time I came to know my mother's first cousins, their last names were Boom, De Brask, McIntyre, Murray, Steele, and Walker; only their brothers "Pony" and Clarence Acuña remained unambiguously Mexican American.

Reflecting on the extent to which my grandmother and the other women in her family had internalized the belief that it was better to be Anglo than Mexican—better to be Mary Douglas than María Velarde—provides part of the answer to why she thought I was demeaning her by saying out loud, among close friends who already knew it anyway, that she was of Mexican ethnicity. But it still didn't seem fully to explain the depth and persistence of my grandmother's anger toward me. It did, however, serve to make me angry at her in return. In the 1960s and 1970s, when there was a great surge of Chicano political activism in this country, I became very judgmental toward her and my other relatives who tried to put as much distance as they could between themselves and the struggles of *La Raza* and the efforts of Cesar Chavez to unionize farmworkers. Either they ignored the whole thing, or they'd talk disdainfully about how awful "those Chicanos" were. How could they not see that the struggle had to do with them? How could they not say, there but for an Anglo last name go I? How could they not sympathize? How could they be so disloyal to their own people?

Almost as if to try to make up for what I saw as their betrayal of their cultural identity, I began to explore it. I'm barely a Chicana: I was not raised in a Mexican American community; my skin is white, not olive; my Spanish is halting and sounds (except for the swear words and bodily parts language) as if I learned it in school as an adult, which I did. Being an Anglo woman is no trick for me; all I have to do and say is nothing and that's who I am. But the awareness of the way in which racism causes the kind of internalized self-hatred that plagued my grandmother and plagues my mother still, and of the way in which it indirectly damaged me by causing my grandmother so abruptly and inexplicably to pass out of my life, made it increasingly impossible for me simply to ignore that part of me that is Chicana. I set about to learn about Mexican American history and culture. I took a job as dean of San Diego State's branch campus in Calexico, a 98 percent Mexican and Mexican American community directly on the Mexico-California border. I was there because I wanted to do what I could to see to it that kids raised, like my grandmother, on *la frontera* had a chance to learn about and take pride in their cultural heritage and not learn to hate themselves for it. I wanted them to be proud of who they are.

Ironically, all the time I was making such a point about the need to be proud of who you are in terms of your ethnic and cultural identity, I was mired in self-hatred of a different kind, for I was a lesbian passing as straight in this little rural Chicano community. At the time, I didn't even see the inconsistency of being angry at the women in my family for pretending they were Anglos while simultaneously pretending to the world that I was straight. A few years later, after I was fired from another deanship when it was rumored that I was a lesbian, I found out that just because you think you're passing doesn't mean you are. And if you are passing, you're probably not doing so as thoroughly as you think, so it doesn't mean that someone won't out you at any moment.

It was that realization that finally helped me identify the missing piece of the puzzle about my grandmother, to figure out what else might have been involved that, when added to her internalization of bigoted attitudes toward Mexican Americans, might have caused her pain profound enough to explain her irreversible rejection of me. It dawned on me that even though my grandmother had dark skin, dark hair, dark eyes and spoke English with a pronounced Spanish accent, so that everyone who encountered her could tell she was of some kind of Latino—if not specifically Mexican—ancestry, *she thought she was passing* as an Anglo lady, Mary Douglas. So, when I told our friends in the car that day that she was "Mexican," I was not just reminding her and them of the whole set of negative characteristics she and they probably believed Mexicans have. I was also, in effect, outing her, revealing what she believed was her hidden secret. And so I was, in effect, committing an unpardonable act of betrayal.

I don't know if this is really what happened, but it might have been. For the first time, I have a way of looking at my grandmother's reaction that makes sense to me: because of her internalized self-hatred of her own culture, she had spent the last thirty years of her life thinking of herself as Mary Douglas, an Anglo lady (and quite a well-to-do one at that since the oil business had been good to Shorty Douglas). And she was the mother of Nina McAlister, clearly an Anglo lady, and grandmother of Linda Lee (for Robert E.) McAlister (even more clearly Anglo, for she didn't even speak Spanish), and she got to believing this so much that, in her mind, she thought she *was* passing. Only she wasn't. I knew that there was no way my grandmother could pass as an Anglo, so in saying she was Mexican I knew I wasn't saying anything that everybody in that car didn't already know.

And I was right about that. But it never occurred to me that my grand-mother might have believed, mistakenly, that she was passing. I was wrong about that. So my unpardonable sin was to reveal what she believed was a secret, even though it was not, thereby outing her, even though she wasn't really passing, except in her own mind.

Actually, when I was working in Calexico, I encountered quite a few Mexican American women of my mother's generation who seemed to be-have in ways quite similar to my grandmother. They were Chicana women who had married prosperous Anglos and who liked to drive around Im-perial Valley in their big cars, join the country club, and serve on boards of various charities, thereby making it clear that they really thought they were somebody and lording it over other Mexican Americans who hadn't achieved this status. Some of these women sported platinum blond hair and made sure they were always called by their full name, Mrs. Smith or Jones or whatever the appropriate Anglo name was. It was quite clear that the spirit of *La Malinche* was alive and well in Imperial Valley.[2] The difference between these women and Mary Douglas was only that they were still liv-ing in the Mexican American communities where they were born and raised, so there was no way they could completely fool themselves into thinking that they were passing as Anglos. But Mary Douglas lived in an Anglo milieu for the last fifty years of her life and there was no one to pro-vide her with the kind of reality check she would get if she still lived in Needles.

Once during my five years in Calexico, I had a business acquaintance who, like me, had one Mexican American grandparent, but in his case it was a grandfather, so his last name was Olivas and he was readily seen as a Chicano. Somehow it came up in conversation that my great grand-mother's birth name had been López. The next time I got a letter from him it was addressed to Linda López McAlister because he mistakenly thought that my middle initial "L." stood for López. I liked it so much I started calling myself that, dropping my middle name Lee (an artifact of my father's family's southern roots), and eventually I changed my name legally to Linda López McAlister. I did so for a number of reasons. In Calexico it was a good idea to let people know that I wasn't "just an Anglo"—that is, that I wasn't totally identified with the Anglo hegemony that held virtu-ally all the power in Imperial Valley. But even after I left there I continued to use it because it sometimes helps keep people from "whitewashing" me, as they're understandably prone to do.[3] It ensures that I won't pass as 100 percent Anglo myself.

What do these stories have to say to us about identity and the current debates about its fixity or fluidity? In the 1990s it became fashionable, at least in postmodern academic circles if not in "the real world," to argue that all aspects of identity are fluid and changeable. My grandmother seems to have thought so, too, in that she seems to have thought she had traded her original ethnic identity in for a new one. And, indeed, there may be no limits to the identity you may imagine yourself to have or no limits to the ways in which you can try to assume a new identity by means of language, culture, dress, behavior, and so forth. But, as in my grandmother's case (and in the case of my sexual identity), thinking you're passing does not make it so.

Well, maybe it's just that she (or I) didn't try hard enough. What if Mary Douglas had bleached her skin, lightened her hair, and taken classes to remove the last vestiges of a Spanish accent from her speech? Or what if I had entered into a heterosexual marriage and had children and never had anything to do with sexual or emotional attachments to women? Would we then successfully pass as Anglo (or straight)? Maybe so. But would those be our identities? I don't think so. To pass implies that you are successfully fooling people into believing that you are something you are not. But there is a world of difference between successful passing and *being* the new identity.

For one's identity actually to change you have to go beyond successful passing and become someone different from who you were. Here I suspect the parallel that I've been assuming to hold between ethnic identity and sexual identity may break down. Let's look at the two cases separately. What would have had to happen for my grandmother's ethnic identity to change? Would such a change really be possible? And if so, would it be within her power to effect? It seems to me that not only would she have to be able to do the things that would be required to pass perfectly, but she would also have had to come down with a case of amnesia so thorough as to eradicate all traces of the language and culture in which she was raised. She could still know Spanish, but she'd have to have relearned it as an adult, for example. And the same goes for all the cultural values she carries with her. Is this possible? Maybe in extremely rare cases. But even with severe amnesia people don't usually forget their language. At any rate, it's not something that's likely to happen very often and not something that one could intentionally bring about oneself. And though my grandmother actually spent more years as Mary Douglas and living in the Anglo world than she spent as María Velarde, and that clearly changed much about who she was, what she was like, it did not make her stop being a Mexican American. Claiming the identity is not enough if you don't have the bio- logical and cultural history to back it up.

Sexual identity seems to me to be somewhat more fluid, if no less complex a matter, than ethnic identity. If you're doing everything you need to do to pass successfully as, say, straight, but you know that your sexual and affectional needs could be better met by someone of your own sex, then you're passing. But sexual desire is itself sometimes an inconstant thing, subject to change in ways we don't always expect. Look at all the lesbians who thought they were straight for years and then began to desire women. Look at people you know who used to be lesbians but who now consider themselves bisexual or queer. It seems obvious that change is possible here and that thinking you've changed your sexual orientation is a lot closer to actually changing it than thinking you've changed your ethnic identity is. It's not clear that either of them is something one can change at will, but a change in sexual orientation doesn't seem to require the same wholesale change in language, culture, and tradition that changing your ethnic iden- tity would require.

But if ethnic identities are nearly impossible to change, how is it that I have the right to identify myself as a Chicana? Am I justified in so doing, or is this merely a case of appropriation of an identity that I have no right to? Here I am, not visibly a Chicana, with English as my primary language, raised in an Anglo community. What right do I have to think of myself as a Chicana, given the fact that my childhood and most of my adult life have been in the Anglo community? Some might accuse me of appropriating this identity for the cachet that it might give me or for some possible ad- vantages it might have accrued to me at a time when so-called "minori- ties" were perceived as getting preferential treatment in some areas (a prac- tice that seems to be rapidly dying out as the twentieth century comes to a close). What would give me such a right? Clearly if I had been born to Mexican American parents, lived in a Chicano community, and spoke Spanish, I would have that right. Even if I didn't speak Spanish I would. Even if I didn't live in a Mexican American community or speak Spanish but had Mexican American parents, I would. So the question becomes what about having only one Mexican American grandparent and only learning a little Spanish, and only sharing in some of the cultural traditions? Is that enough? To which my answer is, "It depends." I think there has to be some biological connection to make the identity claim legitimate—at least some of your relatives have to be themselves Mexican American. A

Finn with generations of Nordic ancestry would lack the necessary biological basis for making such a claim, for example. But while a biological
connection of some sort seems to me to be a necessity, that alone is not
enough to sustain the claim. It justifies the possibility of making such an
identity claim, but it doesn't ensure that's either how you will see yourself
or how you will be seen.

What more is needed? I think it's some kind of an emotional and/or
a political impulse. I have a second cousin in Needles who is actually
"more" Mexican American than I am in the sense that it's her mother, not
her grandmother, who is Mexican American. She, too, has an Irish last
name and doesn't "look" Mexican. When she writes she signs her letters
"Your Okie Cousin, Sharon," alluding to her father's side of the family. My
father's from Oklahoma, too, so I could identify that way as well as she
does, I suppose, but I don't. Nor do I think she has ever entertained the
idea of trying to keep alive her Mexican American heritage in herself or
her children. She doesn't seem to value it at all. Part of the difference between us is, I think, that she has had no experience such as the one that I
had with my grandmother that would make it important to her to see herself as Chicana. But it seems to me that the difference is also a significantly
political one. It's important to me, and apparently not to her, to express solidarity with the Chicano community. It's as though, in our situations, we
both have the option of so identifying but one of us is politicized in that
direction and the other one is not. So while it may be necessary to have
some biological grounds for a claim to be entitled to identify as a Chicana,
it's certainly not sufficient. Despite having less "Mexican blood," I'm a
Chicana, while Sharon is not because she's not interested in being one.
She's perfectly happy to be in the position my mother was—that is, to pass
as an Angla. I don't make the claim of being a Chicana for any gain or advantage that might accrue to me from "minority status." I'm not doing it
out of some romanticized notion of the exotic; I have lived in this community and felt at home there. So I don't feel I'm appropriating anything
to which I don't have a right and a commitment.

What have I learned from these stories? At a very personal level I have
found an explanation of my grandmother's rage that makes it comprehen-
sible to me after many years of confusion, frustration, and sense of loss. I
have learned how damaging it can be to yourself and others to try to pass
as something you are not. I have learned that changing one's identity may
be harder in some respects than it is in others and that each kind of identity needs to be thought about separately rather than lumping them all to-

gether. And it has made me want to honor and embrace all those aspects of my identity that are important to me while bearing in mind that some may change over time. I now identify as a lesbian of mixed race/ethnicity. Angla, Chicana, lesbian, Catholic—I refuse to deny or ignore any of them. I am grateful to my grandmother for giving me the occasion to reflect on these issues. I only wish I had been able to do this before her passing, which I still grieve.

ENDNOTES

1. See Carey McWilliams, *Southern California Country: An Island on the Land* (New York: Duell, Sloan & Pearce, 1946).
2. *La Malinche* is the indigenous Aztec woman who became the lover of the conquistador Cortéz and is seen as both a traitor to her race and the mother of the new mestizo race of Mexicans.
3. As Marilyn Frye did.

> [I]t is the experience of light-skinned people from family and cultural back-grounds that are Black or another dark group that white people tend to dis-believe or discount their telling of their histories. There is a pressure com-ing from white people to make light-skinned people be white. . . . [A] friend of mine to whom I have been quite close off and on for some fifteen or twenty years, noticed I was assuming she is white: she told me she had told me years ago that she is Mexican. Apparently I did not hear, or I forgot, or it was convenient for me to *white*wash her. ("On Being White: Thinking to-ward a Feminist Understanding of Race and Race Supremacy," in *The Politics of Reality* [Trumansburg, N.Y.: Crossing, 1983], 114–15)

I am the friend she was referring to there.

• 3 •

My Father's Flag

Kim Q. Hall

> There's a truth that I am desperate to make you understand: race is
> not the same as family. In fact, "race" betrays family, if family does
> not betray "race."

Mab Segrest, *Memoir of a Race Traitor*

Sometimes I wonder whether it's just me or whether there really are
more Confederate flags these days. No matter what part of the United
States I am traveling through, I always see one. Many friends have had to
suffer through car trips with me during which I point out and rage against
every Confederate flag I see. These flags provoke strong reactions in me.
They always anger and scare me, and sometimes they make me sad. My
problem with Confederate flags is I know all too well what they mean.

Whenever I think about what it means to have grown up white and
female in the South, I remember my father's Confederate flag. For a large
part of my childhood, my father's flag hung on the wall in the basement,
and even though the basement was not a frequently used room in our
house, it was impossible not to notice that flag whenever one went down
there. For most of my childhood I was afraid to descend the basement stairs
alone because I was afraid that a man or a ghost would be waiting for me.
When I did summon enough courage to walk down those steps and peer
cautiously around the corner, I would find myself face-to-face with that
red flag with the blue cross and white stars.

My fears were like the fears of many children who are wary of dark,
shadowy rooms, but there were (and are) many reasons for little girls and
women to be cautious and fearful in a world of men. Fear has been central to the meaning of whiteness in my life: fear of miscegenation, fear of
nonwhite others, fear of being disowned, fear of hurting members of one's

29

family in an attempt to be honest, fear of what one will discover in one's white self if one looks too closely. When I was a child, adults would try to assure me that there were no ghosts or bad men in the basement, but there were ghosts down there, and they demanded my allegiance.

Today, my father's flag beckons and stands as a reminder of who I am supposed to be in my father's eyes. That flag looms in my childhood memories, though I cannot recall exactly what I thought of it as a child. I suppose it would be easy for me to write about how that flag outraged me, but the truth is I don't think I consciously attached much significance to it then. My father's flag was simply (and not so simply) there, like the stereo over which it hung, and on which I remember hearing bluegrass, fifties music, and "Carry Me Back to Old Virginny." Still, my understanding of whiteness has been shaped by my relation to that flag. My understanding of myself as white has been shaped by my relation to histories of racial conflict in the southern United States, histories symbolized most powerfully, for me, by the Confederate flag.

Whenever I tell some southern white people about how much I hate Confederate flags, about how I perceive displays of Confederate flags as acts of hate regardless of the intentions of the people displaying them, they often disagree with me. For these southern white people, the Confederate flag represents not slavery in the Old South but pride in southern heritage. One group that strives to defend, preserve, and pass on "southern heritage" is the Sons of Confederate Veterans (www.scv.org). They beseech other southerners (especially southern men) to defend "My South, My Dixie," and to proudly display the confederate "Battle Flag." However, my question is, Pride in *whose* southern heritage? I've never seen southern people of color flying Confederate flags in their yards, displaying Confederate flags on the bumpers of their pickup trucks, or wearing Confederate flags on their baseball caps. In the southern town where I grew up, white men displayed these flags most frequently. I can already hear the white southern objection to what I've said, the white southerner who knows someone who knows someone who knows a person of color who "doesn't have a problem" with Confederate flags. Perhaps I have had narrow experiences, but I see connections between contemporary displays of southern pride through Confederate flags and constructions of white identity in the new South.

The Sons of Confederate Veterans and other southern defenders of the Confederate flag never hesitate to claim that the Civil War was about "Yankee taxes" imposed on the South, that there were black soldiers who fought for the Confederacy, and that the "true meaning" of the Confederate "Battle Flag" is the Confederate soldier's commitment to hard work, family, respect, sacrifice, duty, and religion (Christianity). It is perhaps no small coincidence that the values attributed to the Confederate ancestor echo the values of hard work, religion, and family that are intrinsic to the New Right's political agenda. The "theocratic Right" in the United States has a long history of using religion to mobilize white people to oppose movements toward economic and social justice. As Suzanne Pharr (1996) writes:

> By the 1990s, the growing racialization of issues such as crime, welfare, immigration, and affirmative action enabled the Right to mobilize white people to support its anti-democratic agenda. Also effective was the covert use of sexism (exemplified by the Promise Keepers) to organize men to assert hierarchical domination, and homophobia to organize heterosexuals to redefine and dismantle civil rights and liberties. (42)

The Right has been very effective in mobilizing white people's fears of nonwhite others, men's fears of women, and straight peoples' fears of queers by representing these groups as the source of economic and social problems in the United States. Similarly, white southerners who appeal to the values of the Old South in their defense of displaying the Confederate flag in the New South appeal to white fear in generating support.

For my father, the Confederate flag represents a South that defended itself and its way of life in the "War of Yankee Aggression." It represents his relation to the men in our family who did not own slaves but who did fight for the Confederacy in the Civil War. My father does not view the Confederate flag as a racist symbol, and he blames white supremacist groups such as the Ku Klux Klan for misappropriating the flag. Like many southern white men who are proud of their southernness, my father is haunted by the Civil War. Indeed, the Civil War is still fought in the South. It is fought in objections to including a monument for Arthur Ashe on Monument Avenue in Richmond, Virginia, among monuments for various Confederate heroes. It is fought with Confederate flags on pickup trucks (usually in the rear window beside or above the gun rack), and it is fought in the way the word *Yankee* comes out of southern mouths like it was a piece of spoiled food.

My father collects oral histories of our family and tries to determine who in our family did what during the Civil War. I want to know this too, but our reasons are different. I want to know who in my family did what to whom. I want stories about the women in my family. I like to imagine that someone in my family protested racism and supported abolition, but these are the stories I don't have. For the most part, I wonder about my need for these stories of resistance.

When my university education and subsequent jobs took me far away from home, some members of my family said, "Don't forget where you came from." For me, home is a place of belonging and pain. It is a place that I know better than anywhere else and a place where there are people who have known me for my entire life. However, home is also a place where I am no longer who I was, a place where my strangeness sometimes makes me suspect. My memories of home are marked by my father's flag in the basement; the black woman who cleaned our house and baby-sat me and my brother and sister; the all-white community swimming pool; adults (not my parents) who reprimanded me to "act white" when I misbehaved; the part of town where black people lived; the Mexicans, Black Indians, and African Americans with whom I worked "pulling tobacco" one summer; the African American girl who became my friend when I went to camp one summer. Home is the place where I first recognized racial difference and what it meant to be white and female. But home is also a place where I am sometimes my father's enemy, a white woman who has been "brainwashed" by "Yankee liberals" in my university education, a white southern woman who has lost most of her accent, a white southern woman who is disloyal to the values of Confederate ancestors and who has, thus, forgotten where she came from. My father wants to pass on to me his pride in our southern heritage, a pride symbolized for him in the Confederate flag. However, whenever I look at a Confederate flag, I don't feel pride. I feel shame and rage and fear, and in these moments I betray my family in my refusal to be a good southern white woman. In those moments histories of fear, rage, shame, and pain mark the distance between me and my father.

I am often told that I could be a member of the Daughters of the Confederacy and the Daughters of the American Revolution since I have male ancestors who fought in both wars. A woman's membership in these organizations is established through the male line of her family. No one seems to care very much about the women in my family history beyond the fact that they gave birth to sons who carried on the family name. The women seem to drop off the pages of the family history after their child-bearing years. I once heard a story about one of my male ancestors who married a Cherokee woman and lived in a cave, but I can never get many details about this woman. I was told that her daughter didn't like to talk about the fact that she was part Indian. I hesitate to mention her in this essay because I don't want to be another white woman who mentions Native American women in her family as if that somehow saves me from the sins of racism and whiteness. I am reminded of Chrystos's (1988) words— "Please don't ever again tell me about your Cherokee great-great grandmother"—but I would not be speaking honestly if I pretended that my knowledge of her has not affected me (66).

Many southern white people from Appalachia have ancestors who were native women. The fact that one of my ancestors was a Cherokee woman reflects the realities of the history of the frontier, a history of white men who moved west.[1] Romanticized portrayals of relations between white men and native women are abundant in contemporary media (e.g., Disney's *Pocahontas*). But whatever the actualities of these relationships might have been, the presence of native women in white people's family trees is a symbol of white male colonial expansion and conquest. Yet this seems to be only part of the story. Native women were more than victims of white male conquest. I want stories in which these women are remembered as subjects of their lives and not used as objects to appease white guilt. I wonder about the other stories I don't hear, the stories that people in my family have chosen to forget over time, the stories that have not been preserved and passed on. The meanings of whiteness in my family are shaped, in part, by what is remembered and by what is forgotten. The story of the Cherokee woman in my family shows how southern white identity is defined through erasing and distorting the lives of nonwhite people.

The Confederate flag is inseparable from white patriarchal ideas of family and nation, and it is one site where constructions of whiteness, southernness, masculinity, and sexuality are entwined. For me, the meanings of the Confederate flag reveal the extent to which my membership in white southern womanhood is contingent on remaining a good, dutiful, loyal daughter. The Confederate flag is a symbol of racial and sexual dominance. Whatever else white men who fought for the Confederacy defended, they also defended the existence of plantation slavery and white patriarchal authority in the South.

In my hometown there is a member of the Klan who flies a Confederate flag on a flagpole beside his house. Because he lives on a main road, his flag is seen by many people. My father once told me a story about a time when African Americans boycotted businesses in our town after the

Klan marched down Main Street. As a result of their boycott, the Klan was prohibited from marching through the town. There is a particular brand of southern pride and nostalgia for Old Virginia that is characteristic of many white Virginians, and many white southerners are angry at the Klan for giving the Confederate flag a bad name. However, the history of white racial dominance is always present in a longing for the Old South, and the Confederate flag is a symbol of that history and of contemporary racism.

Many well-intentioned white southerners are able to take pride in their southern heritage only by burying their shame surrounding the realities of slavery and other forms of racism in the South. However, it is precisely white shame and denial that must be acknowledged and dealt with in order to resist constructions and performances of whiteness that perpetuate racist regimes. In downplaying or forgetting the realities of racial violence that have conditioned white privilege in the Old South, white southerners assert their position as innocent people who are merely interested in knowing about their culture and preserving their heritage. Associations of whiteness with innocence permeate many white people's representations of ourselves. In this particular case, innocent white southerners who want to know more about their heritage are pitted against the guilty, bad white people who are in the Klan, and class is often used to mark the difference between these two groups. In this discourse, middle- and upper-class, educated white southerners are portrayed as the defenders of southern culture, while members of the Klan are portrayed as uneducated white rednecks who give the South and the Confederate flag a bad name.

When southern white people associate displaying the Confederate flag with taking pride in southernness, whiteness becomes synonymous with southernness. In other words, exhibiting pride in southern heritage is one site where white people perform and make meaningful a white identity. White, class-privileged southern men are represented as white and as men in relation to subordinated others: white southern women, women of color, men of color, and "white trash." White southern women are characterized as white and as women in their uncompromising loyalty to the men and children in their family and to the South. Even the stereotypical southern manners and passivity expected from white, class-privileged southern women become ways of firmly establishing one's whiteness and distance from "white trash."

Flags, like whiteness, symbolize "the power to include and exclude groups" (Frankenberg 1997, 13). My father's flag now hangs over a rafter in an outdoor shed. It is barely noticeable. As I look at the tattered and faded fabric, I am reminded of the possibilities of change.

ENDNOTES

1. Conversation with Dr. Patricia D. Beaver, director of the Center for Appalachian Studies at Appalachian State University and coauthor (with Darlene Wilson) of "Transgressions in Race and Place: The Ubiquitous Native Grandmother in America's Cultural Memory," in *Neither Separate nor Equal: Women, Race, and Class in the South,* ed. Barbara Ellen Smith (Philadelphia: Temple University Press, 1999), 34–56.

WORKS CITED

Chrystos. "I Am Not Your Princess." In *Not Vanishing.* Vancouver: Press Gang, 1988.

Frankenberg, Ruth. "Introduction: Local Whitenesses, Localizing Whiteness." In *Displacing Whiteness: Essays in Social and Cultural Criticism,* ed. Ruth Frankenberg. Durham, N.C.: Duke University Press, 1997.

Pharr, Suzanne. *In the Time of the Right: Reflections on Liberation.* Berkeley, Calif.: Chardon, 1996.

Growing Up in Little Rock

Amy Edgington

Several times I have heard white women, who, like me, grew up in the South in the days of segregation, tell a common story. Typically, a woman tells of how she once sneaked a drink from the "colored" fountain and discovered, to her surprise, that the water "didn't taste any different." From that moment she began to doubt what she'd been told about Black people. And she often claims that because of this early experience, she'd never treated Black people any differently from white people. I've heard and read this tale with few variations often enough to recognize a mythical quality about it. Like many myths, it is both a starting place and a stopping place: it begins with a powerful truth that it then distills into a simple, comforting form, like an overstuffed sofa that invites us to lie down and take a long nap.

In working against racism, it is crucial for white people to realize that we share humanity with people we have been taught to view as inferior and to learn that the way the world is ordered is not fair. But too often white people believe that once we face the issue of race on a personal, moral level, we have dealt adequately with the problem, as though one sip from that colored fountain vaccinates us against racism. This myth discourages us from moving to another level, where we might begin to notice that the water in those two fountains does indeed taste different. We simply haven't acquired the taste buds to notice, because growing up in a world owned and run by white people has dulled our senses.

I feel fortunate to have been born in 1946 and raised in Little Rock, Arkansas. Many women from other times and places have told me they believed when they were growing up that white racism was something happening elsewhere or long ago. I am glad I never had this privilege. The dramatic civil rights struggles taking place around me made me aware, even as a child, that just being born white made me an agent of racism. Whether they took pride in it or not, southern whites of my era knew that even if they were poor, they were at the upper end of a caste system based on race.

My own myth involves a bus, not a water fountain. When I was about ten years old, integration was a hotly debated topic in our town prior to the historic desegregation of Central High School. My parents were privately strongly in favor of integration. To them it was a matter of morality. Little Rock was considered a moderate city in the South, partly because it had "peacefully" done away with the Jim Crow law that forced Blacks to ride in the back sections of the city buses. The peace, however, was more like an unevenly armed truce, with a single law on the side of the Black community and the threat of violence, condoned and abetted by the police, on the side of the white community. The result was that even though I rode the bus twice a day, I had not yet seen a Black person move to the front of the bus or a white person sit in the back.

One blistering August afternoon when I got on the bus with my mother, she took the only seat left in what was still labeled the white section. Tradition dictated that white children in this circumstance should stand throughout the ride or sit on the mother's lap. Suddenly something I had done countless times seemed outrageous to me. I was tired and hot; I didn't want to stand for another hour or to be held like a baby. I looked at the back of the bus where there were several empty seats.

Anger at my own dilemma shifted to moral indignation. I knew what the law said. I understood that fear kept Black people from sitting in the white section. The tension in their bodies, their suppressed voices and downcast eyes, the uniformed white bus driver whose thin veneer of jocularity demanded submission—these things I could grasp intuitively as a child in a world ruled by adults. But what kept white people from sitting in the back? I figured it could only be prejudice. It dawned on me that each time I did what I was supposed to do, everyone assumed I agreed with bigotry. I spotted a Black girl a few years older than I was, boldly strode down the aisle, and sat in the empty seat next to her. I did not speak to her, or even look at her after I'd sat down. I sat there, thrilled with myself, braving the glares aimed at me from passengers in the front of the bus, heart thudding for fear the bus driver might stop and put me off the bus, as I had seen him do to Black people he considered "uppity."

By the time I got off the bus at our stop, I had nearly nominated myself for sainthood. I thought that Black girl would remember me forever as the first tolerant white person she'd encountered. But my mother sat me on a bench at the bus stop and gently brought me down a notch or two.

"First," she said, "I'm proud of you for trying to do the right thing. Second," she added, "I don't ever want you to do that again." She passed on to me that day a parent's terror for her child in a potentially explosive situation and the fear that made her too passive to risk expressing her views to white people who disagreed with them. But I do give her credit for the things she made me think about. Did I realize, she asked, the danger I had put the Black girl in? She had taken a far greater risk than I had by remaining in the seat next to me, instead of moving to sit with another Black person and leaving me the seat to myself, as tradition demanded. There was no way the Black girl or even the white people could have known that it was not my intention to make her give up her seat. I had given her no choice but to face possible violence or certain humiliation. I had never really thought about her feelings at all, except to expect gratitude.

Later, my involvement in civil rights and my efforts to make connections across racial lines in high school and college were tentative. I was still determined to do what I saw as right, but I was more aware of the limitations of my moral vision. I often closed my heart because I was afraid I might do or say something racist or thoughtlessly put Black people at risk. I was no longer sure at all that I could do anything right. I felt stuck on that bus where there was no moral place to sit or stand. Guilt was keeping me from learning anything useful or doing anything effective. It's ironic that white people speak so often about being burdened by our guilt. Our guilt may cause us intense discomfort, but it is people of color who bear the burden of white guilt, since it causes white people to collude with racism and to avoid or lash out at the people we believe are making us feel so guilty.

In 1969, I tried to get as far away as I could from Little Rock, thinking that racism was a regional problem and that the only way I could avoid being part of the problem was by leaving the South. I had studied German in college, and worked and saved for a year afterward. My parents gave me a plane ticket as a belated graduation present; so, at twenty-three, I packed my bags and headed for Europe.

The privilege of travel gave me the experience of having to learn the rules of another society from scratch. I became aware of equally complex, unwritten rules that governed my own society, rules that no one seemed to notice or question. I discovered, to my astonishment, that many of the students and a wonderful professor I admired belonged to one of several factions on campus labeled communist or socialist. I thought some of their ideas impractical, wrong-headed, or contradictory, but I gained great illumination from a viewpoint that made class and economics primary. For the first time, I understood politics as something that affects people's daily lives.

I discovered that as an American I had enormous power and privilege coupled with equally vast ignorance cultivated by media and schools that deliberately treat the rest of the world and its peoples as if they were mere scenery or servants, either literally or in the form of military or business "interests." As I read works by authors such as James Baldwin, Malcolm X, Angela Davis, Ann Moody, Ralph Ellison, and Eldridge Cleaver, I started to understand that as a white person living in America, I had inherited a dangerous combination of privilege and self-centered obliviousness toward people of color. I was an imperialist within my own country.

Travel also gave me insight into how racism and colonialism operate outside the United States. I was particularly struck by the example of Ireland, a nation that must surely have been the testing ground for England's harshest methods before its heyday as an imperial power. I knew about the military occupation in Northern Ireland, but I was startled to learn to what extent all of Ireland continues to be kept in economic dependence and exploited as a source of cheap labor, much like former colonial nations of the Third World. This led me to think about how much the economy of the South has functioned like a colony within U.S. borders, how the North had profited from, colluded with, and encouraged slavery. Later, industries were lured south, with local bond issues that paid to build factories, with low taxes and wages that insured that most of the profits would flow back to absentee owners in the North. Bosses told white workers that if they let unions in, Blacks would get their jobs. While factory owners manipulated fear and prejudice, Jim Crow laws were set up to ensure that Blacks remained "in their place," yet most white people in the South still failed to prosper. More than a hundred years after the Civil War ended, the Dixie states lagged far behind other regions of the country in health care, education, and income, for Blacks especially, but also for whites. This was not a sign of congenital southern stupidity, and it was no accident. I began to understand that racism exists because it is extremely profitable for many white people and because even the poorest have been made to fear that they would be worse off economically without it. Clearly, racism was far more than a regional problem I could move away from. No wonder I had failed in approaching racism as a personal moral issue.

My thinking about race during the late 1970s and early 1980s was affected by working with primarily white feminists and lesbian separatists where I lived in northwest Arkansas and the Bay Area of northern California. We began the crucial process of telling our stories and trying to listen to each other's experiences. What constrained our thinking were the unwritten rules of feminism, which assumed that the experiences of middle-class white women defined gender and sexism and which attempted to rank oppressions, with sexism first and worst. The rules just didn't seem to fit the real women I knew, who, like myself, brought multiple identities through the collective door. Women who talked about race, class, anti-Semitism, age, or disability were labeled divisive if they were not willing to chop off pieces of themselves and put them in order—vaginas only, in the front row.

Once we realized that sisterhood could not be created just by hanging a "Women Only" sign on the front door, we demanded endless explanations from women of color, who grew tired of being unpaid teachers. Many of us turned the truth—that we could never experience racism on our own bodies—into an excuse to stop trying to understand. Confrontation and burnout split us into smaller groups—working-class lesbians, lesbians of color, disabled lesbians, old lesbians, Jewish lesbians—finding in such groups a limited haven. But meanwhile, sodomy laws were passed, antigay initiatives were launched, "reverse discrimination" suits were filed by white men. I asked myself whether focusing so much energy on politics as it affects individual behavior wasn't as misguided as approaching racism as simply a personal moral issue.

Books by women of color and some white women—many of them Jewish—who were rewriting and expanding feminism, lesbian politics, and antiracist work, helped me think beyond individual responses to racism. I found much that challenged me and much that confirmed my own disease with white feminism. I learned that all oppressors use similar tactics, that the majority of women and many men in the world experience multiple oppressions, that most of us who are oppressed also experience being someone's oppressor at some point in our lives. Oppressions do not operate independently or order themselves into a neat hierarchy; they interlock like a three-dimensional web. It was pointless to argue which strand came first or was strongest, because every strand of oppression reinforces the others and tightens the web, whether that particular strand touches your own life or not.

From my own experience, I could agree with women of color that forming political alliances based on identity alone had limited value. For over a year I belonged to a group of lesbians with disabilities: it felt liberating to bring all of myself into that room and feel safe for two hours every week. But our stories revealed widely different experiences with disability. In addition, some felt being poor or female or lesbian or Jewish had impacted their lives more than disability. But we stuck together, because if we bonded only with those who shared identical experiences, we would split into even smaller groups. Those who had suffered the most numerous oppressions might find themselves in a "group" of only two or three or someone might wind up talking to herself. We would become totally ineffective. We also noticed that common experiences do not necessarily make common goals, and as we began to work with women who were temporarily able-bodied and with men who had disabilities, we learned that we might find support for our issues in spite of differences.

This period of my life brought me back to my home town at age forty, where I had to get on a Little Rock bus for the first time since early in 1969. I was not conscious that day of remembering the many times I had seen African Americans humiliated or how frustrated and helpless I had felt. I associated my sense of dread with the discomfort and tedium of one of the same long routes I had ridden since before I could talk or walk. I took my seat in the middle of a bus with fewer passengers than in the past, but as had frequently been the case in my childhood, most riders were African American, female, middle-aged or older. Although I had noticed buses driven by African Americans, some of them women, this driver was a white man. I numbed my mind for the first ten or fifteen minutes. Then my immediate surroundings crept back into awareness: all around me were the voices of African American women in full tone; laughter, hilarious or ironic; bodies and gestures loosened in sharing tales.

This was kitchen table talk, the kind African Americans never used to let slip in front of white people when I had grown up here. At one point the driver stopped on his route and went into a small laundromat. Buses often stopped when they ran ahead of schedule, but this time the wait stretched out. The women around me began to swap theories full of increasing mockery, about just what might be taking the driver so long, openly poking fun in front of white people at a uniformed white male figure who had once been a powerful tin god in the South. Eventually, he returned and the ride resumed; conversation continued to flow around me, and I found that my heart was cracking open, letting a ten-year-old's impotent outrage and shame flow out of my body and seep silently down my face. I turned toward the window to hide my tears. Too little had changed in Little Rock, but this had, and my tears were tears of gratitude. I was thankful for a glimpse of intimacy, strength, and spirit that had been carefully nurtured and shielded from white eyes for so long in the South; I was far more grateful that getting on the bus no longer meant unavoidably casting my lot with racists. I had long known that African Americans, particularly women much like those around me, had done most of the dangerous work that made this possible, starting with the Montgomery bus boycott, continuing with the unnamed African Americans who braved their way up the aisle to the front of every Little Rock bus, including the driver's seat. But now I was feeling in the roots of my being what I owe those civil rights warriors: certainly, I was not the intended beneficiary of their struggle, but nevertheless, they helped create a world where I have the chance to become a true adult instead of remaining a child who must do what white men dictate.

In spite of the distress guilt causes white people, it's probably more comforting than gratitude. As a white person I had been taught to feel superior, but true gratitude is a humbling experience. It's also demanding. It awakened a need in me to become worthy of what I have been given. Collective white guilt included a childish arrogance that told me people of color should be grateful for gestures of tolerance on my part. It's ironic to me now to remember how white people who backed integration constantly encouraged other whites to be more tolerant, as if we were the ones suffering from our racist attitudes. Everyday in Little Rock, when I interact with African Americans where I work or in any other public place, I am amazed at the tolerance shown to me as a white person, given the history of this town and this country, and at the degree of openness I often receive. I am learning also not to expect openness, to accept the fact that many people of color cannot and will not tolerate the real possibility of any foolishness or worse on my part. That response is certainly not "racism" on their part. And it does not let me off the hook in the least.

Ironically, collective white guilt allows each individual white person to maintain a child's pose of innocence and powerlessness—"It started long before I was born. It's not my fault. There's nothing I can do about it anyway." To grow up, I must replace collective guilt with the concepts of collective privilege and collective responsibility. I need to acknowledge and learn from my individual mistakes, while recognizing the advantage white skin gives me, regardless of how I behave.

If you are trying to think and act beyond an individual approach to racism, I have some suggestions. Wherever you live, start a reading group centered on works by and about people of color that would help antiracist white people understand racism and our stake in fighting it. Begin a group of women and men who are willing to monitor and analyze local news stories for incidents and attitudes that create the climate of hatred leading to acts of violence, and take the further step of writing letters to the editor that counter this hatred, to make the voices of justice-loving people heard in our communities. Learning and doing go hand in hand, and the mind and heart follow where the body leads.

• 5 •

Pinay White Woman

Linda M. Pierce

It is very easy for me to pass as white. My whiteness has always been an asset, a quality for which I was actually praised. Whiteness is an asset for anyone white, and it is reinforced through the usual processes: socialization, economic opportunities, the media, and various discursive practices. However, the value of my whiteness was also explicitly reinforced by the Filipino side of my family, who held me on a pedestal because of my appearance, as if I had accomplished some incredible feat for the *pamilya* (family). The colonization of the Philippines by white America only compounded the pre-existing structures that connected socioeconomic status to the degree of sun-darkened skin. But years of white "First World" leaders, the dominance of America the white superpower, and equation of whiteness with technological advancement, military supremacy, and economic development all helped convince my *pamilya* of their racial inferiority. My brown-skinned family wanted to be white because they saw the supposed superiority of whiteness enforced daily on every television show, film, billboard, and magazine. They viewed America as the "land of the free" where money, power, and whiteness are conjoined. Five out of seven of my *lola's* (grandmother's) remaining children married white spouses and had light-skinned children.

Since my mother is the lightest of all the children from the Ramos/ DeLeon-Douglas clan, it was no surprise that I turned out so light. She was a very famous movie star in the Philippines, admired for her white skin and her "statuesque" 5'4" frame. At the tender age of thirteen, she was declared Junior Miss Philippines in a pageant that narrows down the finalists to the Ten Fairest, of which the winner is crowned *Snow White: The Fairest of Them All*. After migrating to the United States, my mother learned that the virtue of white skin was more useful for assimilating than for standing out. Once the *pamilya* laid eyes on me and found me to be markedly different from my much darker, obviously Asian/Pacific Islander–looking older

45

brother, they declared me the next Miss America, the one who was des-
tined to carry on my mother's legacy.

My *pamilya* wanted to be able to point to a Miss America from their
family, yet the very reasons why they were sure I could achieve such
heights were the same reasons why I could not really be the first Filipina
American Miss America. My Filipina ancestry is enough to make me not
purely white, but my white skin similarly disqualifies me from being a *pure*
Filipina. I exist between identities, and my light skin makes it easy for me
to pass for white. As a result of white skin privilege, I succeeded easily in
the American public school system. I have never knowingly been marginalized or seen as suspect because of my racial appearance. I have never had
a problem buying makeup to go with my skin tone. I have always been able
to take for granted the privileges associated with white skin. I have darker-
skinned Filipina cousins who are much prettier than I, cousins who my
family could never see as candidates for the first Filipina American Miss
America because their features are "too" Filipina.

Although this worship of American whiteness fostered an intense internalized oppression by teaching my *pamilya* to hate their brown skin and
to strive to become more "American," it did not result in the obliteration
of our Filipino culture, which somehow managed to survive in a state of
contradiction. The *pamilya* could rationalize white superiority if they considered themselves white. The more children they had who looked like
me, the easier it was to convince themselves of this truth, this progress to
whiteness. What they could not deny, however, was the language, the food,
the cultural ways and familiarities that made them Filipino. My *pamilya*
could not separate themselves from the culture that was embedded in their
sense of being and that made them intrinsically non-Western: their value
systems, including the importance of a large and close-knit clan, the de-
centralization of parental authority, their ways of interpreting events, and
their experiences as colonized "Third World" people. We all lived the du-
ality between white and Filipino, and in my own experience, the contradictions remained unexplained for years.

The *pamilya's* great claim to whiteness was grounded in the white
American soldier who married my grandmother and lived with her for
over twenty years in the Philippines. He learned to speak Tagalog "like a
native" and exemplified the perfect combination of all things good in both
cultures. He spoke the language, ate the food, lived in the culture, yet he
was still white, American—civilized. His self-imposed "exile" to the Philippines, a response to his own family's staunch disapproval of his brown-
skinned bride, would last only as long as dual citizenship was an option for

his children. Shortly before my mother's twenty-first birthday, when her right to American citizenship would expire, she was whisked away to America along with as many members of her immediate family as U.S. immigration would allow. In the land of plenty my mother was taught that only savages eat with their hands, that famous Filipina movie stars are only second-rate compared to glamorous Hollywood actresses, and that eating the blood of the pig was an abomination, not the enjoyment of a delicacy.

Along with our admiration for our white American grandfather, the *pamilya* centered around the Filipina matriarch, Linda Maura Ramos DeLeon Babista Douglas, the grandmother after whom I am named. My grandmother prides herself on her American citizenship, compares her life in the United States to the squalor and poverty she remembers in the Philippines, and measures her success by her American children's material wealth (though poverty increased in the Philippines with the influence of American capitalism). Yet she exists within a Filipino subculture, speaks Tagalog to her children whenever possible, eats only Filipino food, shops only at the Filipino market, and only wears traditional Filipina gowns at formal occasions. The *pamilya* raised their young boys, brown and white alike, to expect a princely inheritance in the traditional patriarchal manner. We all went to church on Sunday to worship a white, male savior who promised to save us from ourselves.

While my early years of childhood were filled with these strange, often confusing contradictions, the U.S. military eventually shipped my father off to a new location, tearing my mother, my two *kuyas* (brothers) and me away from the subculture in which we had been so immersed. With the exception of occasional phone calls between California and New York, my mother had no one with whom to speak Tagalog. My brothers and I lost the language we had only begun to acquire. Our Filipino culture seemed to wash away with each new relocation (to California, Alaska, New York, and finally Washington), and my identity as a Filipina American faded as well.

Although my mother was able to preserve some of our cultural traits, I can see now how every public and private institution was working against her efforts. I remember coming home from school while in the sixth grade and correcting her English grammar or pronunciation according to what my teachers had taught me. My mother always confused plural and singular, could never remember to pronounce the *h* in words such as *think* and *thanks*, and kept pronouncing a *p* sound where there should've been an *f* and a *d* where there should've been a *t*. For the longest time I thought that she simply did not understand basic grammar. I remember wondering why she could not just stick to the rules of standard English. After all, these rules were easy enough for me. I was very hard on my mom.

My mother must have felt she had to deny her culture to gain respect from her twelve-year-old daughter. For a long time, she made a conscious effort to pronounce things "correctly" for the sake of her children, and she always apologized whenever she was corrected by one of us. The older I got and the more I succeeded within the public school system, the more my relationship with my mother worsened. My father, whom I was said to resemble, did not understand the reasons for my tense relationship with my mother. I did not understand, either.

By the time I reached high school, "Filipina American" became only a box I checked when applying for grants or schools, a way for me to claim minority status and to possibly get an extra benefit from affirmative action while remaining safe in my shroud of whiteness. I had no problems reconciling this claim. My mother was definitely a Filipina, and I had grown up surrounded by a brown-skinned family, though that all seemed so far away from me. When I started college I made a feeble attempt to join the Asian Pacific Islander Student Union, located within the Ethnic Student Center. I am not certain whether my motivation to join was out of feelings of obligation, curiosity, desire to reconnect with my heritage, or less admirable reasons, such as a desire to be fashionable.

My interest in joining these clubs quickly waned. I felt unwelcome there, alienated because of my white skin and angered by the assumptions that others made about me. I became bitter as I saw brown-skinned, fourth- and fifth-generation "pure" Asian Americans, who seemed so Americanized and even more disconnected from their culture than I was, immediately embraced by other students of color while I was marginalized. I felt *discriminated* against when they ostracized me because of my white skin, since on the inside I was really one of "them." I wanted so badly to be accepted as "Filipina," but I was not willing to acknowledge my "American" side and the white privilege and complicity that came with it. Much later, I would begin to recognize the need to create a space where I could live with both my appearance and my culture, but at the time I was unable to piece the two together without a dissonance that left me defensive and confused.

From this confusion, I began to actively seek out new theories and information. Through my college education I was eventually introduced to feminist and critical, postcolonial perspectives.[1] The feminist perspective I first learned, insofar as it was very mainstream and American, only furthered the distance between my mother and me. My naive criticisms of her "domestic slavery" failed to consider her within her traditional, cultural context. Mainstream American feminism helped to question some of the structures that have contributed to the marginalization of women, and to consider how

I myself might be complicit in oppression, but it did not help me understand other, interlocking systems of oppression, such as racism and colonialism.

Postcolonial theories made me question everything that had served to construct what I considered to be my "self," including my political and ideological notions, my family background, and my own legacies of institutional and internalized racism. I began to recognize the ways in which I have played a role in the colonization of my mother, and I began to understand how my actions continued to limit her in terms of her language and dialect, her cultural frame of reference, and the general standard for becoming "Americanized" that I had embodied and helped to enforce. As I remember my twelve-year-old desire to correct my own mother, I realize how imperialism works to physically and intellectually "whitewash" cultures and how children are strategically manipulated in the colonization of their parents.

Through reading postcolonial theory, I began to understand some of the questions, conscious and unconscious, that I had as a child. Why was my *pamilya* so proud of my whiteness? Why were all the Filipina women I knew married to American servicemen? Why did my mother mix up her plurals and singulars? Why did we have such a tense relationship? I began to see parallels between my personal history and the experiences of others who have been colonized by white America and Western Europe. I began to question my socialization, my mother's socialization, the way in which two generations of Filipina women were "colonized" by American servicemen, and the systematic cultural genocide that has influenced my mother's family line. My *kuyas* and I had already lost the language, some of us had lost the color, and we were all losing the value of our brown-skinned cultural heritage. The realization was frightening. In another two generations, the *Pinay* line in our family could be completely eliminated.

Ironically, it was these new understandings that initially led me to reject my Filipina identity. I stayed away from claims to a "woman of color" identity because I feared that my white privilege denied me any real claim to my *Pinay* culture. I felt that my whiteness created a boundary between me and them that was too huge for me to overcome. Indeed, it seemed as if only an act of white privilege would enable me to overcome this boundary. For me, trying to bridge the gap between "white" and "Filipina" seemed too risky. I didn't trust myself, and I worried that I might become too comfortable in a space where discomfort necessarily defines me. I feared that I might just emphasize the cultural understandings that I shared with Filipinos and downplay important differences, especially my white skin privilege. I was afraid to face my Filipina culture because I resemble members of the dominant culture who benefit from the oppression of Filipino/Filipinas. My skin reveals my complicity.

While this was the first time I felt really proud of my culture, it was also the first time I felt so ashamed of my whiteness—ashamed of what it had done to my *Pinay* culture, ashamed at what I had done to my mother. My white skin, my very existence, was the most glaring evidence of my complicity, and as much as I wished it away, it wouldn't disappear.

I felt confined by whiteness and found it ironic that my older brother, who was seemingly uninterested in our culture, was the one who did not inherit white skin. However, every time I begin to entertain such thoughts, an awareness of privilege reminds me that his brown skin brings him face-to-face with everyday acts of racism that I can easily avoid. My brother and I were brought up the same way, but the dominant culture has taught him to hate his skin while it has taught me to value mine. Every girlfriend he has ever had has seen him as simultaneously exotic and exempt from his culture. After some comment his fiancée made about "Asians," he had to tell her, "Hey, *I* am 'Asian.' Our kids will be *Asian.*"

As I became more comfortable identifying myself as a Filipina American, I began to develop one-to-one relationships with other *Pinoy* and *Pinay* students. While the Asian population on campus was large, the Filipino population was cloaked, and *Pinoy* students were eagerly searching for others like them. Lost amid many Asian groups, the Filipino students wanted to be recognized as a unique but connected culture. I began to look at the group in a new way. As I recalled my sense that I was a victim of reverse discrimination, I realized that I had reacted out of ignorance about my own white privilege and out of a desire—created by privilege—to remain in the center at all times. I finally understood why other students of color might be suspicious of me, make certain assumptions about me, or not embrace me as a full member of their culture. I am not part of that culture. I exist outside the culture, on one of Gloria Anzaldúa's (1987) "borderlands"— with traces of my Filipina heritage blended through and beneath my white skin. I understand the ignorance behind the use of terms such as *reverse racism,* which assumes that there is no real power imbalance, no "dominant culture," and which denies the unavoidable structure of American racism.

Through my relationships with other *Pinays* and *Pinoys* I have come to understand that I am not alone. Before, I felt alienated from my peers because I thought the internalized racism, and the confusions and contradictions between white and *Pinay,* were unique to my *pamilya.* The realization that I was not alone—indeed, that both "pure" and "mixed" Filipinas experience internalized racism—and that "purity" itself is a racist notion provided me with a path into the culture in which I had felt marginalized. This knowledge gave me access to a community and a space in which my mixed blood could flow freely.

Meanwhile, my immediate family had planned a trip to visit the *pamilya* in California after a long absence. My heightened sense of cultural awareness and deeper appreciation for what it means to be *Pinay* made it possible for me to put my disturbing realizations aside and look forward to reconnecting with the clan, but what I found was an environment reminiscent of my contradictory childhood existence. One of my uncles, a police officer, had adopted the overt racism that appears only too frequently in law enforcement while simultaneously acting as the department liaison and translator to the Filipino community. One of my *titas* (aunts) was always complaining about getting sunburned, and when I said, "I thought Filipinos were used to the sun as a result of growing up in a tropical climate," she replied, "Are you kidding? Filipinos hate the sun; that's why they carry umbrellas around everywhere they go—*they don't want to get any darker.*" All of my relatives agreed that this was true, but none of them was willing to take this analysis to the next step and consider explanations for this phenomenon. When I asked why Filipinos don't want to get any darker, all I heard was "I don't know," "Just because," or "That's just the way it is."

The preference for light skin does predate colonization, and it refers to economic situations where darker-skinned people were usually peasants who worked in the sun all day. Nevertheless, colonization perpetuates, exacerbates, and takes advantage of this hierarchy. The notion that lighter skin makes one somehow "less" Filipina, and concurrently more American, is more colonial propaganda designed to subjugate, and often annihilate, the colonized culture. I could see where the seeds of my own brainwashing had been planted. Now my task is to work to prevent its flowering.

Because of the way ethnic groups are managed in the United States, there is an insistence, through such things as government census bureaus and all federal and employment documents, that people "choose" one identity, rooted in ethnicity, by which to define themselves. The insistence on one identity, even "woman of color," places limitations on all *mestiza* or mixed-blood populations and, in turn, affects our self-definition. I am not simply "white," and I do not see myself as a woman of color. With less bitterness and guilt and more comfort with myself and my larger sense of purpose, I realize that I am a white-skinned woman with a *Pinay* heritage, a white-skinned Filipina American who is not entirely comfortable in either culture yet who exists in both. I live in the borderlands, where my perceptions of reality are shaped, where I construct my sense of self, and where I feel most at home. Gloria Anzaldúa (1987) describes living in a borderland as being "in a constant state of transition":

> Every increment of consciousness, every step forward is a *travesía*, a cross-
> ing. I am again alien in new territory. And again, and again. But if I es-
> cape conscious awareness, escape "knowing," I won't be moving. Knowl-
> edge makes me more aware, it makes me more conscious. "Knowing" is
> painful because after "it" happens I can't stay in the same place and be
> comfortable. I am no longer the same person I was before. (48)

I know that I can expect to change my understanding of myself many
more times throughout my life, that these transitions are a part of the
process of locating oneself, interrogating one's position of privilege, and
working through the pain of alienation. The pain serves as a good reminder, a check against becoming too comfortable and against the desire
to forget about all of the complications.

ENDNOTES

I am grateful to Rosanne Kanhai, a woman of color from Trinidad who was teaching comparative literature, postcolonial theory, and women's studies at my university, for being (for me) a model of non-Western academic success. Rosanne was
the first academic woman I heard pronounce a *d* sound where I had been taught
in my Western education that there should have been a *t*. She bridged the gap that
had been constructed in my mind between Western interpretations of success and
Western stereotypes of Third World women. Rosanne also helped me understand
my responsibility to use my white privilege. She helped me face the pain.

1. Influential in my learning and thinking were Gloria Anzaldúa (1987), Carlos Bulosan (1943; Evangelista 1985), Chrystos (1988), and María Lugones (1990).

WORKS CITED

Anzaldúa, Gloria. *Borderlands/La Frontera: The New Mestiza*. San Francisco:
    Aunt Lute, 1987.
Bulosan, Carlos. *American is in the Heart*. Seattle: University of Washington
    Press, 1943.
Chrystos. *Not Vanishing*. Vancouver: Press Gang, 1988.
Evangelista, Susan. *Carlos Bulosan and His Poetry: A Biography and Anthology*.
    Seattle: University of Washington Press, 1985.
Lugones, María. "Hablando Cara a Cara: Speaking Face to Face." In *Mak-
    ing Face, Making Soul/Haciendo Caras: Creative and Critical Perspectives by
    Women of Color*, ed. Gloria Anzaldúa. San Francisco: Aunt Lute Press,
    1990.

Section Two

Performing Whiteness

• 6 •

The American Celebration of Whiteness

Judy Scales-Trent

Sometimes I think cab drivers are the worst. White cabbies, I mean. There must be something about being in their own car and sitting in front that is like being in their own home, being in charge; there is something that makes them feel entitled to say absolutely anything that comes into their head.

This is my latest white-cab-driver story.

It took place only recently when I moved from my rambling old house in the city to a townhouse in the suburbs. With my son grown and gone, my beautiful city home felt too big. And after eleven years, I had learned more than I ever wanted to know about grubs, snow thatch, and bores in crabapple trees! A small townhouse where someone else would worry about snow and grass and shrubs seemed just right.

Although it was a little disorienting to move from the city to the suburbs, much remained the same: my friends were still close by, and I wouldn't have to look for a new doctor or dentist, bookstore, or car repair shop. Or cab company.

So this day I had called the same cab company for a ride to the airport; I was in one of the same cabs, with one of the same drivers. And I was preoccupied with my thoughts: would the house sitter be able to get into the house? Had I remembered to put the right files in my briefcase? Did I bring the plane ticket?

And that's when the cab driver decided to chat.

"So," he said. "I see you've moved to the suburbs."

"Yes," I replied, trying not to encourage a conversation.

But he was unstoppable. "So why did you move?" He looked at me through the rearview mirror, then gave me a conspiratorial smile. "Trying to get away from the blacks?"

My heart stopped.

"Oh, my God," I thought, "this fool thinks I'm white!"

55

Because I am a black person with white skin, this happens to me a lot. But no matter how many times it happens, it always knocks me out to realize that someone thinks I'm white and that he is therefore safe to say any racist thing he wants. I had thought that I was paying eighteen dollars for a ride to the airport, only to discover that I would pay much more than that for a ride on the AmeriRace Express.

People often ask me what I do in situations like this. Well, it varies. Sometimes I'm speechless; sometimes I leave the room; sometimes I respond; sometimes I cry. And sometimes I do all of the above. But every time, every single time, I have to first pick myself up off the floor after that knock-out punch before I can do anything at all.

This time, I answered calmly and quietly: "Well, that doesn't make any sense at all, does it? How could I leave *myself* in the city? Is there some reason I should try to get away from my family and friends? Why on earth would I do that?" The cabdriver had the grace to turn red in the face and apologize. He also had the good sense not to utter one single word for the rest of the trip. And I was left to sit in silence in the back of his cab and try to put myself together . . . try to get ready for my next encounter with white America . . . try to find the strength to keep on keeping on.

Have you ever seen that Eddie Murphy skit where he puts on white makeup and gets on a bus to see what happens when white people think there are no black people around? In the skit, as soon as the last black person gets off the bus, the white people relax and start talking and laughing with each other. The bus driver turns on music, they bring out food and drink, and they start dancing. It's a party! Well, as an unwitting, unwilling spy on white America, I can tell you that this is not exactly what happens when my darker brothers and sisters "leave the bus." But it's close. For many white Americans *do* relax when they think there are no black people around: they relax enough to say what they really think about black Americans. And I have come to understand that when white Americans make these comments, it is indeed a celebration, for they are celebrating their whiteness and their privilege and their power.

Eddie Murphy got to take off his white disguise. Sometimes I wish I could, too. But I can't. Like other black Americans with white skin, I will always be faced with situations where white Americans, thinking I'm white, too, feel safe to make racist comments in my presence.

Social scientists call this a problem of having to manage stigma that is not visible.

I call it living with a sore that keeps getting dirt in it, a sore that never seems to heal.

· 7 ·

The King of Whiteness

Chris J. Cuomo

*T*his is a story about a white girl who chooses whiteness over knowledge. It is a story about me. When I say that I'm white, I supposedly mean there are no folks of color in my family or my family's history, as far as I know, or as far as it matters. In the naming of my own racial identity, I apply a detestable principle, the one drop rule, to tell you that I am pure—with no colored blood. But where does a family history begin?

Is my application of the one drop rule so seamless? What if, contrary to fact, I had a Great-Aunt Ella, married into the family, who was Chinese, who taught me her language, and who loved me like a grandmother?

More likely, my dark immigrant family arrived in New York uncertain of their social status yet certain that their skin was the color of olives, not eggplants (as they came to describe the skin of this country's former slaves). How many generations, how many miles from the center of the city does it take to whitewash ethnicity? I claim the generations before me as "white," as though that's the way those peasants from Sicily and Czechoslovakia saw themselves. As though whiteness were timeless.

Stories of how the Irish "became" white aside, it's clear that Europe matters. No matter that the successes and superiorities associated with Europe were the results of nearly accidental combinations of technology, luck, and evil. Europe set out to rule the world and made the pale face a sign of power, money, and knowledge. This despite other associations of that face with stupidity, aesthetic inferiority, and moral decrepitude.

What is this identity "white" that marks my body, that I (here, now) cannot help but take as a name? I am white, yet I believe that in some other universe of meaning and power, things could be otherwise. In my own life, I don't really know how to make sense of this belief.

Since I've come to understand whiteness not as an attribute or quality but a category that maintains its own power, I've longed for an alternative.

57

Just as I moved myself (or so it seemed) from straight girl to lesbian so many years ago, I wish I could abandon whiteness—this form of personhood that signifies oppression—and forge an identity that marks, with the simplicity of a name or a haircut, just how fucked up I think racism is. There are moments when I agree with those who say that the elimination of racism requires a flight from whiteness. But to where? When I consider what it would mean to not be white, my political conscience becomes uneasy (wannabe!), and my imagination fails me.

I think: I can only hope for a miracle. I wonder: What do I stand to lose?

Yes, this is all about me. That's a white people habit, a middle-class habit—to think and talk as though we deserve being the center of attention. It's downright American. But what does it really matter what my identity suggests to the world, as long as the lives of people who aren't white, rich, or "normal" are trashed by the norms of race, class, and gender?

I hate when men say they are not really men. What a lie, I think. If you're not really a man, why can't I see your inability to reside in privilege? Shouldn't the whole world be able to see your discomfort in conforming to the rules of manhood? Let's see your privilege crack you in two! Let's see you give it up, brother! Until I know you're for real, don't tell me you're not really a man. You have no idea.

My friend Suzanne was born a man. Before she became Suzanne, the guy she was participated fully in manhood. He was married, had children, and was a member of the U.S. Air Force (Suzanne tells me that many transwomen are former military men). Suzanne became a woman in ways that are visible because she felt like a woman inside—in ways that only she knew. *I hate when men say they're not really men.* When Suzanne says she didn't feel like a man before, I don't mind. Something has convinced me that before she became a woman, Suzanne could not abide the norms of manhood. As a man, they were destroying her.

Whiteness is not destroying me. I can't say that I always felt white, because I just always felt normal. As soon as I knew that not everyone was white, I knew that I was at the top of the heap. I knew that I had been born lucky. There were other ways that I felt like a freak, different from the people around me. I would rather read than play kickball. I could communicate with animals. I thought prejudice was bad, and I protested and sometimes cried when my family told racist jokes. None of these qualities ever made me feel that I was not white. Lucky.

Whiteness, education, and money help get me just about everything I want in the world, including love and good health (knock wood). Although I feel little kinship with most white people, whiteness is not a prison house for me. It is easy to be white. Do men feel this way about their privilege? Are you laughing at me?

I have very little knowledge about what it means to not be white, and whatever I might have to say about not being white could be said much better by someone who is not white. So what makes me think I have anything worthwhile, anything worth your time, to say about being white? About what I think about my own whiteness?

Wait: In order to say something about whiteness I begin thinking about not-white. Why is that so much easier than thinking about whiteness itself? Because white is nothing. White is everything, and there is absolutely nothing redeemable about whiteness. White is history, context, oppression. And me. I'm white.

But I'm getting ahead of myself. This is a story about the standpoint of whiteness. I offer it to provide some fragments, to add these patterns and contradictions to the narratives we construct together regarding race, gender, and desire. Is it at all worth trying to understand something about race through the lens of gender? You be the judge.

★★★

A drag ball was being held as a fund-raiser for AIDS organizations, and Kristin and I assumed there would be a handful of drag kings among the scores of queens. Kristin is big and beautiful. Her mother is Filipina, her father is from Puerto Rico ("I'm not sure if he's really Puerto Rican," she says, "I was always told he was Spanish"). She arrived at my house in a tailored black suit. I wore my thrift store suit, cufflinks, white shirt buttoned to the neck. Kristin used mineral spirits to apply a mustache to her face. I could get away with just using mascara to highlight my own mustache and sideburns. She showed me a trick—darkening the eyebrows—and we both plastered our hair straight back with lots of hair gel.

Oh, my God, I said.

We look like Chicano homeboys, she said.

Dark sunglasses on, and we hit the street. I felt like Danny DeVito next to Jimmy Smits.

This is who I've always wanted to be, she said.

Shit, I thought, I'm scared.

There is the danger of walking out of one's home dressed like a member of the wrong gender. There is the danger of looking like a hood in a neighborhood crawling with cops. There is the danger of looking Latino in a neighborhood where white yuppies, Appalachians, African Americans, and assorted queers coexist in an uneasy tension. What did I fear? Getting caught.

The car felt safe. It felt right to be cruising through the city, sitting on the passenger side as Kristin drove, windows open, my head bobbing to the beat as Celia Kruz led us into the night. It was when we reached the center of the city that the first miracle occurred.

We slowed for a traffic light. Two African American girls—teenagers—were walking along the sidewalk on my side of the street. By instinct, I smiled at them. I was completely unprepared for the miracle that met me on the face of the younger girl. The smile she gave me in response was completely open and inviting. It was the kind of smile I've only seen on the faces of women who are flirting with me and confident of their conquest. It is not a look that I have ever gotten from or given to a stranger.

She liked me.

I remembered how I looked and realized, she really thinks I'm a guy.

I thought, this is how straight people flirt with each other all the time!

I thought, she does not think I am white, as we drove to the fancy banquet hall.

There is another version of this story—the version in which I make Kristin stop the car, and we join those girls instead of going on to the draggy fags, and I spend the evening making that girl laugh. But I'm not telling that story right now. I'm telling the one that happened in time and space, not in the gossamer of imagination. I'm telling you the story in which the clueless drag king is offered redemption. And refuses.

Drag queens call themselves illusionists. Get close to one, and it's usually easy to see that she's really a guy. Though I create illusions of identity all the time, I didn't think about the power of illusion until I became a brown man for an evening.

The second miracle involved the male gaze. Kristin and I were the only girls in boy drag at this midwestern extravaganza. It seemed that hardly anyone was fixed on the action onstage, as queers milled about, costumed for pleasure. In the dark cabaret scene we still passed. We hung out in the back of the hall, arms crossed, occasionally relaxing the stance to smoke. We watched the parade of monstrous divas sashay to the stage, shaking our heads at the poorly executed lip syncing, taking in the full glory of the long curvaceous legs on the fake ladies. By the time the awards ceremony started, we had found a groove. And who noticed us?

White boys dressed in leather.

The look was clear and direct. Sexual, fierce, but not threatening. I felt like a curious, inexperienced boy, peering into the edge of a culture that I longed to join. I felt like an adventurous seasoned fag sizing up the possibilities. I thought some white leather daddy could show this homeboy a very good time, if I were sufficiently willing. This not regardless of the exoticization and arrogance that likely lurked behind that wanting whiteboy gaze.

I thought, I am getting much more action as a Latino than I ever get as a white dyke.

I felt a surge of potential in one of those moments that is ubiquitous in queer experience, where gender seems to melt away and we all are just beings with a wide range of genitalia and facial hair and nose shapes and skin tones and the bodily truths are intoxicating. Squint, and that guy walking toward you has a genderless face. Blink and that tall woman's dark skin is only the play of light on flesh. Close your eyes and there are no signifiers. Just scent and heat and an open range of connection, repulsion and transformation.

The third miracle began with the phone ringing. We were in position near the back wall when a service phone near Kristin's head began to ring. Phone ringing? In the middle of a party? Is someone calling?

Kristin moved to pick up the phone. With a sudden perception that crackled I became aware of the uniformed staff patrolling the party. Were they protecting the queers, or monitoring us? As Kristin brought the phone to her ear they descended on her—white men in uniform ready to wrestle this troublemaker to the ground and prevent the inappropriate use of a service phone. They were MAD. They were SERIOUS. And they assumed that the colored guy picking up the phone was up to no good.

It broke my heart to see, in that flash of a moment, Kristin's look melt from pure cool to startled nervousness. What, she said. What did I do wrong?

Later I thought that maybe it had been the Virgin Mary on the phone. See, stupid (she said), I gave your sorry ass, your lucky ass, three visions of truth. Three visions of a reality that your lazy white self has the privilege and misfortune to ignore every damn day. She provided the miracles, but I failed. I never got to hear her Semitic wisdom, and I blame the white men in uniform.

This is who I always wanted to be.

★★★

The bartender notices me from the corner of his eye and immediately makes clear his distaste, his suspicion. He thinks if he ignores me, maybe I'll go away. I think, He thinks I'm Latino. I think, He's being mean to me. I think something bad is going to happen.

I know that when I open my mouth I will commit myself to a gender. I realize that with a lilt and a smile I can escape back to whiteness and exit this moment of awkward fear. Or I can test out my boy voice and remain threatening to this $5-an-hour bartender.

I could also just avoid the whole dilemma by pulling out my money and pointing to a beer. But I don't.

I smile sweetly. I find my feminine register. I let him see my whiteness and my gender, let him see that I'm not scary. I order a whitegirl beer, and in gratitude and solidarity I leave a big tip.

I commit the original sin of whiteness. I let go the knowledge.

• *8* •

"Whitie" and "Dyke":
Constructions of Identities in the Classroom

Laurie Fuller

What determines the meanings of whiteness in my life? As I sit here at the computer, the screen is white and the words I write are black, and I notice that whiteness structures everything that I see. And for you, reader, the page is white; the words are black. How does whiteness on the page and beyond it structure your reading of this text?

In the context of my life at present, I have been wondering how whiteness structures my teaching and how I might use my role as teacher to disrupt certain meanings of whiteness. Yet I cannot ask such a question about whiteness as though it was removed from my other identity positions. My response to this interrelationship is to try to make sense of my context and experience in relation to race, gender, class, sexuality, and other identity positions. (To clarify, I am using the terms *identity* and *identity positions* to refer to the ways that people understand their own and others' race, class, gender, sexuality, and additional markers about themselves, such as size, age, etc.) Here, I will describe two different classroom situations, one a large Introduction to Women's Studies lecture course at a land grant university in the Midwest and the other a smaller (twenty-student) upper-level women's studies course on Lesbian Culture at the same university. Both classes were composed of mostly white students. In both classrooms, some identity positions were explicitly discussed and some discussions of race took place, and also in both classrooms, an implicit pedagogical goal was to make sense of the identities around which the course was centered, "women" and "lesbians." What I want to focus on in these two situations is the way that students and teachers can construct, through their words and deeds, identity positions as normative and known or as more fluid and context-specific. Perhaps surprisingly, notions of identity as shifting and an understanding of whiteness as a fluid historical identity were more effectively conveyed in the larger introductory-level class. I do not mean to imply that the classroom contexts were strikingly similar. Rather, I want to use my experiences in these two classroom situations to explore some possible reasons why and how identities come to be understood and examined. I am particularly interested in how language can be disruptive and, for example, how (or if) the use of some jarring term, like *whitie* or *dyke,* might draw attention to identity and disrupt its presumed stability.

IDENTITY IN THE CLASSROOM

I believe that in university classrooms, teachers' and students' own understandings of identities as given and fixed, on the one hand, or as fluid and contingent, on the other, reinforce different ways of understanding race, gender, sexuality, and other identity positions. One factor in how the politics of identity get played out in the classroom lies in the terms that mark identities and the ways these terms are enacted. For example, depending on how they are delivered and understood, terms such as *white* and *lesbian* can either stabilize or undercut common understandings of what they are meant to signify. These terms are meaningful only in relation to their surrounding histories and contexts, and these histories and contexts impact their meaning and malleability in the classroom.

The terms that interest me most are politically important primarily in connection with histories of racism, sexism, and homophobia. In classrooms where I teach and learn, terms that describe race, class, gender, and sexuality are always in circulation. Language is one tool through which college and university classrooms can become places where identities come to be seen as context-specific and historical. The words we use shape how we think about the world and ourselves. Therefore, careful use of language to point to how identities are multiple and shifting rather than known and fixed can work against racist and heterosexist assumptions. In my view, my work as a postsecondary educator is to encourage students and teachers to learn about themselves and others in a more open and less judgmental way and also to encourage students and teachers to develop a complex, multifaceted, and dynamic view of how the world works.

Before I go on to discuss how terms such as *whitie* might work in classroom situations, I should make clear another belief about notions of identities that circulate in classrooms. Teachers' and students' conceptions of identities as fixed or fluid have an impact on classroom dynamics. The most basic way I try to explain this in the Introduction to Women's Studies course is that there is no phrase you could make up about all folks who call themselves women without somehow excluding some women. I try in the classroom to come up with some phrase—"All women love bunnies" or "All women love babies"—that will cover all women. Yet it is clear in a large lecture class that there might not be any phrase that could describe all women, even just all women in the room. The point of this exercise is to show that the use of the term *women* in this way excludes some women. So if all women are supposed to love bunnies and I don't love bunnies (but I do; this is just for the purpose of the example), then what? Am I not a woman? Specifically, understandings of identity positions as fixed—"All women love bunnies"—contribute to classroom dynamics in which some students and teachers get othered or are seen as unintelligible as that fixed identity. If you don't love bunnies, then you must not be a woman. Classroom practices that work against fixed identity positions work against othering because when identity positions are under-stood as fluid, there is no absolute and fixed identity position, such as "All women love bunnies," from which to fix someone as other or as "not woman" (Ellsworth and Miller 1994).

I know this seems like a silly example. I believe that its triviality high-lights the insidious capacity of language to fix identities. I don't even need to say *all* women love bunnies to create a fixed and simultaneously exclu-sionary or othering situation in the classroom. Hopefully, no students will get hurt by this exclusion, but this example is indicative of the use of phrases and statements with more impact and more social exclusionary power (i.e., "All women get married and have children," etc.). With this in mind, I want to return to my opening questions about the structuring power of whiteness. Has the term *women* been used here in a way that has implied "white women"? Has my lack of racial specificity implied white-ness? Is whiteness not only structuring the page of this paper but also the terms and language with which it is written?

CREATING LESBIAN CULTURE?

Part of my motivation to make understandings of identities fluid in the large Introduction to Women's Studies course was my experience as a stu-dent in a course where understandings of identity had become known and fixed. The reason this experience stayed with me was because class discus-sions became minimal, and I believe that fact was due to the ways in which understandings of identity became fixed, leaving no room to question or consider multiple or changing conceptions of identity. Moreover, it seemed that many students felt othered by the experience in the course and therefore were silenced. I want to explain this experience more fully so that my conception of fixed identity positions can become clear.

I was a student in a Lesbian Culture course where the classroom dynamics encouraged some participants to speak and to act as though they understood and knew everything important about lesbians and lesbian culture. In the class *lesbian* came to function as a fixed identity. This might seem to make sense because the title of the course was indeed Lesbian Culture. However, it is my contention that during the semester the questions "Who are lesbians?" and "What is lesbian culture?" became so fixed and defined that all those who were unable to fit into those definitions became other, or not real lesbians.

Again I would like to return to the questions that started the chapter, which is a small digression from the current discussion. How is it that whiteness is structuring my use and your reading of the term *lesbian*? It is my experience that the term tends to imply whiteness—that use of the term *lesbian* often refers to white lesbians—unless there is some sort of qualification to include all lesbians no matter what race. I wonder whether *lesbian* is a white term somehow. Of course, the meaning of the term depends on context, who is in the room when the term is used, who is using it and how it is used. I want to explain how I am thinking about the structuring power of whiteness in this essay and in this sort of writing. So I raise the question, when you read the word *lesbian* how do you think about it? Is it structured by whiteness? How do you conceptualize *lesbian*? This consideration of the structuring power of whiteness is part of the backdrop to the ideas of this chapter, especially in relation to the use of terms and their unspoken, unwritten meanings in both classrooms and written articles.

I think the ways in which identities become fixed is a complicated and complex process that I do not pretend to fully understand. However, I feel that I know when it has taken place. I will give my impressions of how and in what ways conceptions of lesbian and lesbian culture became fixed in the course I took as a student. Hopefully, this can begin to point out ways in which this fixing of identities and othering in the classroom might happen. First, the course was a historical and contemporary investigation of conceptions of lesbians and lesbian culture. Looking back, I now think that at least one goal of the course was to define *lesbian*. Some participants spoke and acted as though they understood and knew everything important about lesbians and lesbian culture. In my own head, I named them the Lesbian Knowledge Goddesses. They spoke and pronounced whether someone was woman-identified or male-identified (a seemingly meaningful distinction at the time) and whether she was therefore lesbian or straight, regardless of what the woman herself said. The class dynamics encouraged participants to work to understand what was/is lesbian culture and who were/are lesbians. The Lesbian Knowledge Goddesses had found an important forum, and their knowledge came to be privileged in class discussion as they began to define who was a lesbian and what was lesbian culture. Through the course focus on the meaning of *lesbian* and the Lesbian Knowledge Goddesses' work to outline their own definitions, it seemed that understandings of *lesbian* became fixed. Over the course of the semester discussion dropped to a minimum.

To illustrate how this fixing can take place, I offer an example from class. One day a student was discussing how her first female lover had been with a man at the same time she was with her. This lover vacillated between the two relationships and ended up breaking up with the woman. The Lesbian Knowledge Goddesses instantly pronounced the lover as male-identified. I wondered whether the situation was somehow more complicated than the explanation "She was male-identified" implied. In fact, I felt as though there wasn't enough information about the lover to *know* whether she was or was not male-identified. I wasn't even sure it was so important to discuss (let alone pronounce) the extent to which she was male-identified. But the woman who was telling the story originally, the woman whose lover had left her to be with a man, agreed with the Lesbian Knowledge Goddesses, thus ending discussion.

My experience was that the learning environment was constricted because there was no space in discussions to question or complicate the terms *lesbian* and *lesbian culture,* even though the course was theoretically about understanding lesbians and lesbian culture. Even more to the point, there was no common or commonsense understanding that lesbian culture was being created and re-created in that very classroom. Such a sense of the continual creation of notions of lesbians and lesbian culture might have resulted in discussions about how lesbians are wounded, and mended, when our lovers leave us, or love men, and about how we deal with loss. The class could have been a place to discuss the ways in which lesbians create terms such as *male-identified* to help explain why women leave lesbians and lesbian communities to be with men. Unfortunately, this particular classroom was not a place where such issues were discussed. The pronouncement of male identification managed to shut down discussion and fix lesbian and lesbian culture as something static and completely understandable. I don't think it was necessarily that the Lesbian Knowledge Goddesses were working to shut down discussion and other women in the classroom with their outlining of their understandings. But because the class was somehow working to define *lesbian,* the Lesbian Knowledge Goddesses were able to use the classroom space to create, fix, and maintain their definition of *lesbian.* It wasn't just a one-day affair. Over time their voices and points of view began to take up more classroom space and dovetailed well with one of the unspoken course objectives, to define *lesbian.*

I understand some of the reasons why the Lesbian Knowledge Goddesses wanted to define *lesbian* and *lesbian culture* as fixed and clearly definable. In a homophobic, sexist society, it is useful for lesbians (and everyone!) to know and understand who other lesbians are. Lesbians can also gain a feeling of security with the sense that they know quite a bit about lesbians and lesbian culture. However, a sense of security did not open up discussion in the classroom. On the contrary, it seemed to shut down discussion and fix lesbian culture as static and as something that some knew more about and could therefore explain to the rest of us. Because a sense of security was gained by only a few students, those who knew the meaning of *lesbian* as fixed, and those of us who questioned that fixity seemed unable to penetrate the solidity of their ideas, anyone who did not fit the bill was othered or excluded. Over the course of the semester, class discussion determined who was lesbian and what was or was not important about being lesbian, and there appeared to be no space in the class for different understandings of lesbian.

Again I would like to return to the question about how whiteness is structuring your reading. Conceptions of lesbians and lesbian culture have not been discussed in relation to whiteness in a few pages. Is the use of the term *lesbian* somehow whitewashing your thinking about lesbians? One of the fixing aspects of the Lesbian Culture course was the fact that discussions about lesbians were primary and discussions of all those other aspects of identities, such as race, class, age, and so forth, were secondary. Even though people cannot experience their lives that way, we spoke as though there can be a separation of lesbian identity from other identity positions. This mistake can constrain the term *lesbian,* so that it comes to refer only to lesbians with other "normal" identities such as being middle-class, white, or able-bodied. I realize that the text you are reading may also separate lesbian from other identity positions. I continue to insert these questions and put lesbian in relation to whiteness in order to work against this separation.

The example of defining *lesbian* illustrates one way identity positions can get fixed and how those who are different therefore become othered. The Lesbian Knowledge Goddesses expressed lesbian as an exclusive and absolute category, thereby othering lesbians who are closely bonded with men. Trying to understand and outline who is like us, and how they are like us, can be a useful survival skill for disenfranchised groups. (Isn't it also a good way to identify potential girlfriends? That's a joke as well as a serious comment.) But the way knowledge was created in this context helped create a climate in which it was difficult to raise questions and issues that did not jive with the classroom version of lesbian and left virtually no space for plural and contextual interpretations. If the class discussion, with the help of the Lesbian Knowledge Goddesses, had not so firmly determined who was lesbian and what was lesbian culture, I believe there would have been space in the classroom for more people to participate in *creating* lesbian culture.

It was not just the way the course was set up, to outline and define lesbians and lesbian culture, in combination with the efforts of the Lesbian Knowledge Goddesses, that fixed understandings of lesbian in this classroom. I believe there was also an unreflective use of the term *lesbian*. As my example of "All women love bunnies" was meant to illustrate, the use of terms such as *lesbian* or *woman* in some sort of sweeping and defining way in the classroom can other and exclude those who are outside of the ruling definition. Since the course was somehow about understanding who lesbians are and what lesbian culture "is" (is it just one thing?), there were many discussions in which statements such as "Lesbians separate themselves from men" were uttered as though they were complete truths instead of sweeping generalizations. So, these experiences in Lesbian Culture resulted in rumination about how terms and phrases are used in classroom discussions, about how classroom communication can get shut down, and about the potential for classroom dynamics to contribute to the fixing of identities.

COMPLICATING WHITENESS

This experience made me more sensitive to terms and how they fix identities in classroom situations. As the instructor of a large Introduction to Women's Studies lecture course, I tried to pay attention to the ways that terms and their uses in the classroom help maintain or undercut the belief that identities are fixed. For example, I worked to complicate essentialist conceptions of gender and always to discuss gender as shaped by race, class, and other aspects of identity and social location. One way I did this was to highlight how the term *women* can be exclusionary through the "All women love bunnies" exercise and then carefully explain how language and the exclusion of it works.

I tried to build on the groundwork that I laid with the term *women* by trying to complicate other identity positions. My experience is that most white people do not conceptualize whiteness as an identity. Instead, white people assume that we are really just Americans or humans and we don't need to think critically about being white people because white is just the normal, natural way of being human. Race is something that describes a quality of African Americans or Asian Americans, not white people. This can be seen by asking white people what they think about being white. Their whiteness has often gone unnoticed or experienced as if it were nothing (Dyer 1988). Of course this is not the case for all whites, since white supremacists organize their identity around their race. But it is the very "normalcy" of whiteness that allows white supremacists to see racial outsiders and others. To keep whiteness from getting fixed as nothing or as normal, I use my position as instructor to talk about myself as a white person and to discuss how white privilege structures my life. I also historicize constructions of race by discussing the history of racism in the United States. By constantly referring to whiteness in relation to gender and class and sexuality and so on, I try to make whiteness more visible and to weave it into understandings of other aspects of identity. Moreover, I make efforts to point out how white students and teachers get unearned privileges from whiteness, to help create a space in which we might think about how race and racism circulate in culture.

In my teaching, I often used the term *whitie* to refer to white people. I use *whitie* to refer both to historical figures such as pilgrims and to people alive in the present, such as my family members. When I first developed this tactic, I believed that calling white people *whitie* would be like using a large pointer to underline whiteness and the ways that it tends to go unnoticed by people who believe they are white. I used the term *whitie* when I discussed how selves are contextually determined and how gender identities in the United States are always racialized. I hoped to identify and destabilize understandings of whiteness and to encourage more sensitive and contingent understandings. I also wanted to make available a conception of whiteness that could be explored as an actual historical and social aspect of white people's identities, not as a banner of pride but as a source of meanings, entitlements, and privileges of which we should be critical.

Another reason I began to use the term was because of its historical situatedness. Because *whitie* is a term used by people of color to refer to whites, through which the oppressed refer to the oppressor, it served to highlight for white students the fact that their perspectives are limited. The term *whitie* can emphasize and link whiteness to its particular history of entitlement and privilege from the point of view of people of color, not from the point of view of whites concerned with reverse discrimination and white rights or even from the point of view of antiracist whites. Also, I thought that it might emphasize whiteness as a relational identity that is noticed and derided by people of color. It is not just the normal and natural way of being human. I realize that this term of resistance created by African Americans might lose some of its resistant power if appropriated by whites. Right now, it seems to have the jarring effect that allows it to highlight the myth of white normalcy. However, its effects are dependent on context. My ability to use *whitie* to destabilize is related to my whiteness and many other factors.

Whitie had two original functions for me: to emphasize whiteness and to connect whiteness to histories of racial oppression and privilege. But I was not motivated by these two actions alone. One other aspect of my teaching that you may have gleaned from my "All women love bunnies" example is the use of irony. Part of my motivation to use a term such as *whitie* is the jarring and ironic edge. It is not every day that students see a white woman standing on a stage in front of one hundred people and using the term *whitie* to refer to herself and other whites. I have found that it also has an impact in conversation with white people. Yet, this is not the same among all white people. If you try it, recognize that it matters who uses *whitie* and in what context.

While I am not sure that I was able to make the complexity of whiteness understandable to white students, my use of *whitie* elicited some remarkable responses. Did my use of *whitie* from the insider position make other insiders, such as white students, question their racial identity? Students began actually to refer to whiteness in class discussions, and the classroom became a space in which whiteness seemed to lose some of its stability. This became clear when white students were pushed beyond their comfort levels, and they contested my use of the term *whitie*.

On the day that I used *whitie* to name the pilgrims and other Europeans who came to this land, I asked for anonymous responses from the

students. While my intention was not to alienate the students or make
them feel disrespected, a number of students mentioned that the use of
whitie had disturbed them. I believe that students' discomfort could be seen
as a sign that they were noticing whiteness. I had assumed that it would be
acceptable to use *whitie* to signify myself and other whites because I am
white. But because *whitie* interrupts what students expect teachers to say
about white people, or because I was using the term to point out and emphasize colonialism, the students were insulted. I thought it interesting and
informative that these students (the majority of whom were white) were
offended by my standing before them and referring to myself, my ancestors, and other white people as whities. Perhaps the students were angered
because *whitie* is derogatory slang and they had a history of it being used
against them in a painful way. But certainly, out of my white mouth and as
a name for myself and my white family, *whitie* necessarily means something
a little different than its history of use as derogatory slang. In fact, I took
students' discomfort as a sign that I got what I was hoping for, a little jarring irony to bring whiteness into focus, not to center it again but to make
it available for discussion and as an identity that is relational with privileges,
entitlements, and history.

It is not just the use of a term that created a more fluid understanding of whiteness in the classroom. I believe that over time the classroom dynamics encouraged open questioning of the ways that conceptions of identity positions, such as woman and white, circulate in culture
and in our own lives. It was not that somehow *whitie* moved the class
discussion into a new realm. Rather, it was one tactic for pointing out
how whiteness is like and unlike other racial identities and is related to
particular histories, entitlements, and complicated meanings. One of my
main goals in this classroom was to make understandings of gender always at the same time about race, class, sexuality, and so on. An important aspect of that agenda, with a large, mostly white female student
body, was to highlight the ways that whiteness shapes and structures
gender for white women, just like blackness shapes and structures gender for black women. I tried to emphasize a point described by Sherene
Razack (1998) in her book *Looking White People in the Eye* "that women
are socially constituted in different and unequal relation to one another.
It is not only that some women are considered to be worth more than
other women, but that the status of one woman depends on the subor-
dinate status of another woman in many complex ways" (158). So emphasizing both the *relational* and *hierarchical* nature of identity positions,
such as woman and white, as well as emphasizing the changing and con-

textual aspects of identity were my pedagogical goals in the classroom. I saw the use of *whitie* as just one attempt toward that end.

SEAMLESS SIMILARITY . . . NOT!

Looking back at the Introduction to Women's Studies course I taught in relation to the Lesbian Culture course I took, I began to think about possible ways of working to unfix conceptions of lesbian. If *whitie* helped destabilize understandings of whiteness in the classroom lectures, I wondered whether there might have been a similar term, such as *dyke,* which could have worked in similar ways in the Lesbian Culture course.

Of course, the contexts for discussions in these two courses were very different. Perhaps the only similarities were that they were both women's studies courses and I was present in both of them! Nonetheless, I want to examine these two classroom experiences in relation to one another because I think the treatment of identities in the classroom can be impacted by language. I do not believe that constructions of lesbians and lesbian culture, a subjugated identity position, are seamlessly similar to constructions of whiteness and white identity. My interest in relating these two identities comes from my experiences, which led me to wonder whether there might have been possibilities for making lesbian more fluid in the classroom.

I ask this question about language because I think that the ways in which whiteness gets normalized in classrooms are often very subtle but can be seen as related to the more visible way that lesbian got normalized in the Lesbian Culture course. Often whiteness is just taken to be the normal natural way of being human. It is not discussed and hardly anyone points to the way that whiteness structures identity positions *for whites.* Whiteness then becomes acontextual and all encompassing, the unspoken, taken-for-granted way of being human. Obviously this is not the case with conceptions of lesbian. Nonetheless, it seemed to me that one object of the Lesbian Culture course was to define and outline what *lesbian* means. In the context of a "lesbian–positive" classroom space, conceptions of lesbian culture and lesbians were actually normalized (an interesting thought to say the least). In such a context, perhaps the use of some jarring term, such as *dyke,* might draw attention to lesbianness in some way that destabilizes its fixedness in the classroom. Could the use of *dyke* with its jarring associations somehow have undercut the normativity of classroom understandings of lesbian, like *whitie* helped undercut whiteness?

I realize that there are few commonalties between *whitie* and *dyke*. For example, the history of the terms *dyke* and *whitie* are quite different. *Dyke* has been used by "normal" heterosexuals against those who are understood as abnormal, gay women, and lesbians. However, *whitie* is a term used by people of color to refer to whites, the oppressed referring to the oppressor. I suggest the term *dyke* because it is rarely used in the classroom and because it is transgressive. In some lesbian communities, *dyke* has been transformed from a curse to a term of power, though it can still have a hurtful impact. Both its disruptive history and the contested nature of its reclamation (only within certain circles is the term not considered derogatory) could be useful in unsettling a seamless and fixed conception of lesbian and opening up discussions of multiple conceptions of lesbians and lesbian culture.

This chapter is not about answers to problems. It is meant to provoke thought about how some careful use of language, especially some jarring terms or irony, can open up discursive spaces in which identity positions can be contested and unsettled, and therefore can be less fixed and othering. Are there other practices that can also perform these destabilizations or other approaches to creating contingent and shifting meanings of identities in classroom practices? I'd like to think so.

In conclusion, I invite you to consider the ways in which whiteness might somehow not only structure the page on which you are reading this but the terms in which the essay is written. Can *lesbian* have a meaning that is not normalized by whiteness? Can *dyke*? How about *woman*? Herein lies the incredible structuring power of whiteness within language and terms. Even when it is not mentioned, whiteness can shape meanings and understandings and can be assumed as the normal and natural way of being.

WORKS CITED

Dyer, Richard. "White." *Screen* 29, no. 4 (Autumn 1988): 44–64.

Ellsworth, Elizabeth, and Janet Miller. "Working Difference in Education." Paper presented at the *Journal of Curriculum Theory* Conference, Banff, Canada, October 1994.

Razack, Sherene H. *Looking White People in the Eye: Gender, Race, and Culture in Courtrooms and Classrooms.* Toronto: University of Toronto Press, 1998.

Section Three

Identity and Privilege

· 9 ·

White Ideas

Naomi Zack

*W*hen I first heard about whiteness studies, it was in the context of "white trash" affirmation. I was skeptical of its friendliness to "nonwhiteness" studies and, indeed, to nonwhites. This was because I thought that at least some of the folks who fit the stereotype of white trash also fit the stereotype of "rednecks," a group with members known to be unfriendly to nonwhites; other members of the white trash category were known to object strongly to affirmative action for blacks. I was also skeptical about the friendliness to nonwhites of white folks' public assertions of their racial identity as white. It was my earlier understanding that only Nazis and other white supremacists *made a point* of being white, so it was difficult to believe what everyone in academic contexts seemed to believe when white people asserted that they were white—namely, that they were doing so to express their sensitivity to injustices against nonwhites. I experienced all of this skepticism in the early 1990s, after returning to academia from a twenty-year absence.

Now, after having written and edited several books that examine the culturally constructed nature of American biological racial categories, I have been asked to contribute a narrative to this collection of writings on whiteness. It's going to be an intellectual account because I am not ready to write a personal account of my experiences of whiteness. But, it will still be a narrative because I want to discuss several ideas as I understand them, without the usual scholarly apparatus of specifically cited sources. And, since others who have written about these ideas may have different understandings of them, my (unscholarly) exposition and critique may, despite my impersonal intentions, in the end say something personal about me.

To my mind, the intellectual question is still whether a person of color can completely believe that it is possible for whites to talk about whiteness in ways that are not racist against nonwhites. I remain skeptical about at least the four ideas to which I will devote this essay: the idea of race traitors; the idea of white privilege; the idea of white guilt; the idea of white racial identity. Each of these ideas is employed by contemporary white liberatory scholars in efforts at self-examination on the subject of racism against nonwhites. While I take their good intentions at face value, my skepticism is focused on the broader historical contexts from which these ideas derive their meanings and on present social and linguistic patterns that destabilize what those who use these ideas think they mean.

THE IDEA OF RACE TRAITORS

I believe that the origins of this idea are malign, and it's not clear to me that it can be reclaimed given what is now widely accepted about racism in the United States. During the American civil rights movement(s), some whites supported the cause of blacks for voting rights, equal education, and other civil rights. White southerners who did not want black southerners liberated in the ways in which they were already entitled to be liberated by law called the whites who supported the blacks "traitors to their race"— race traitors. This usage implied that loyalty to whites by other whites was a virtue comparable to patriotism and that membership in a hereditary caste could be betrayed by behavior disapproved of by other caste members. In other words, some behavior by whites was held wrong to the point of being dishonorable and of such importance that it could dislodge a hereditary identity. It is striking (as Martin Luther King emphasized) that the traitorous behavior was not unlawful according to federal or, in some cases, state law, so that support of black southerners in their quest for civil rights often amounted to nothing more than support for an enforcement of federal and state law that already granted them those rights. Thus, the so-called white race traitor was someone who insisted on obeying the law when other members of his or her race insisted on disobeying the law. The treason at issue was, in short, a violation of a criminal code according to the criminals who believed they were above the law.

In principle, then, a white race traitor in this original American sense would be no different from an inner-city gang member who decided to live a straight or square life. Both the white race traitor and the renegade gang member would require considerable personal courage to persist in their behavior, punishment by assault or murder being highly likely.

If a traitor to a nation is convicted and executed, the verdict and sentence may be judged harsh, but most observers do not question the right of the government to bring them about. The case is different with civil rights movement–era white racists and criminal gangs because these groups do not have the right to punish those considered traitors. The context in which such racists and gang members make the judgment that someone is a traitor is skewed, because they do not have legitimate authority to do so. They are not sufficiently important, duly constituted, or powerful to apply the term *treason* to disobedience of their rules. For this reason, the judgment that someone is a race traitor by a white racist is overblown and somewhat bizarre, similar to denouncement by a comic book villain. Why, then, would someone who was seriously committed to racially egalitarian behavior clothe him- or herself in that mantle?

I suppose that a contemporary self-styled "white race traitor" might dignify the mantle by explaining that normally law-abiding white people are so unjust against nonwhites in their daily behavior at home and in institutions that they constitute a conspiring group that, in moral and even political terms, is no different from the civil rights movement–era southern white racists or vicious gang members today. At that point, it would be difficult for me to determine whether the present self-styled white race traitors were serious. Because white racism against blacks remains a serious matter, I would remain skeptical until these people explained to me how exactly, in their understanding, ordinary white folk do form an everyday conspiracy against the well-being and dignity of nonwhites. I would want evidence of some clearly understood and well-documented prosaic facts about ongoing American racism. I would want to hear more than that white people enjoy privileges on the grounds of race, for example.

THE IDEA OF WHITE PRIVILEGE

I am irritated when my students begin essays with references to dictionary definitions because usually the words they have looked up have a history of analysis and discussion by philosophers that is much deeper than the dictionary definition, and I want them to grapple with elements in that history. However, if a word has no philosophical history, it's enterprising to look it up in the dictionary and circumspect to show some awareness of its real-life usage and meaning, also, before making it do some philosophical work of one's own. The last time I looked in the dictionary, the word *privilege* derived from the Latin sense of a private law. It meant a prerogative or exception granted to an individual or special group, or, in modern constitutional law, it referred to rights that all people were supposed to have. In ordinary usage, *privilege* means some special advantage, such as the privileges of wealth, or the privileges of officers, or the privileges of members of the American Philosophical Association. There is no philosophical tradition of analysis or discussion of this word, so it is odd that so many contemporary liberatory scholars now talk about white privilege without benefit of dictionary definition or ordinary usage.

Even in this most racist of cultures, there is no legal tradition that grants special rights to whites so much as there is a present social practice and a past legal history of excluding nonwhites from the privileges assumed to belong to all citizens, in the second sense of the dictionary meaning of *privilege*. The idea of white privilege, then, must be an elliptical reference to the result of discrimination and exclusion of nonwhites. To call the result a privilege, which means a positive, specifically granted absolute advantage, rather than a relative one, clouds the issue of disparities between whites and nonwhites. It makes it seem as though the situation is both worse and better than it is: worse, as though at some time benefits for whites only were explicitly conferred upon them by law; better, because the emphasis on white privilege ignores the discrimination against and exclusion of nonwhites that give rise to the racial disparity.

I do not think that the elliptical idea of white privilege can bear much weight philosophically. It certainly does not add anything to the idea of white race treason. To say that one is a white race traitor because one is against white race privilege is to say that in the sense of the civil rights movement–era American South one would betray the criminal intent of white people because compared to nonwhites who have been discriminated against and excluded, whites are better off. What is left out here is a claim that it was wrong and unfair for nonwhites to have been discriminated against and excluded. There may also be a tacit assumption lurking that whites are better off in some absolute sense when they are only better off relative to nonwhites. That is, if nonwhites were included in general privileges and not discriminated against, the net long-term effect might be more benefits for whites than they have now. Furthermore, the use of the term *white privilege* makes it seem as though white people have advantages and status that only white racists think that they should have. To speak as though these privileges exist puts the comparative disadvantages of nonwhites "in their face" in a way that would seem (to me) to add further insult to injury. At this point it might be objected that some white people feel guilty about the fact that whites are so much better off than nonwhites.

THE IDEA OF WHITE GUILT

Well-meaning white people who style themselves race traitors may feel guilty about what they unclearly view as white privilege. Of course, this guilt has a history in the culture. When Americans were more racist in public than they now are, it was assumed that nonwhites were not as well off as whites because they were inferior to whites in important economic, intellectual, and civic skills. Now that educated whites realize that white advantage is the result of historical racism, their earlier feelings of superiority have been replaced by compassion at injustice, remorse if they ever felt superior or now identify with white predecessors who did, and, in some cases, a discomfort that is called *white guilt*. This guilt is sometimes a sensitive individual reaction to unearned personal benefits, believed unlikely to have been granted if the beneficiary were nonwhite. But, given my earlier analysis of white privilege, the problem here is not that the benefits are unearned but that nonwhites do not have the same unearned benefits. A second source of white guilt is recognition of belonging to a group that is historically guilty of injustice against other groups. This is often connected with ideas of collective responsibility and historical justice, which, although they fuel rich debate, are often not connected to present disadvantages experienced by nonwhites. That is, neither the psychological guilt based on unearned advantages nor the moral guilt based on past injustice entails an awareness of contemporary white moral obligations arising from contemporary racism.

Most nonwhite liberatory scholars understand the main problem of contemporary racism to be institutional racism, a problem to which white guilt is largely irrelevant. The idea of institutional racism defines racism as something about nonwhites, whereas earlier ideas of racism, from which the idea of white guilt descends, were mainly about whites. It's useful to consider several of those earlier ideas of racism to understand this difference in who racism is supposed to be about. Between about 1950 and 1970, white people who thought nonwhites were inferior to them were called *bigots*. As integration became a more widespread public reality, whites who thought that American society ought to be integrated sometimes felt obligated to assert that they were not *prejudiced* against nonwhites and did not *discriminate* against them, because they were *tolerant*.

These ideas about race relations filtered out social realities of race. Bigotry originally meant attachment to a creed, religion, or party, and it was never made clear how it came to be extended to racial aversion. Prejudice presupposes that one will at some point make a judgment. But why should racial difference be a subject of judgment or automatically associated with contexts of judgment? The idea of discrimination presupposes that the objects one accepts are present alongside the objects against which one will discriminate. That is, strictly speaking, "discrimination" requires some prior comparison. Nonwhites, however, have often been completely excluded from contexts in which whites interact among themselves, and it is this exclusion that precludes the possibility of nondiscrimination—because it excludes the possibility of discrimination. The idea of tolerance suggests that there is something otherwise unacceptable or objectionable that one will "allow" to remain or against which one will not react negatively, perhaps by shutting down critical faculties or suspending one's standards. All of these earlier ideas used to show that whites were not racist presupposed as normal a certain amount of ill will or contempt for nonwhites. To say that someone was not bigoted, unprejudiced, did not discriminate, or was tolerant conferred moral praise on a person for not participating in the ill will or contempt of others for nonwhites. None of these ideas contributed much to an understanding of the effects of racism on nonwhites. The contemporary idea of institutional racism, by contrast, implies an idea of white responsibility that is more relevant to the situation of nonwhites than ideas of bigotry, prejudice, discrimination, and intolerance. And the present idea of white responsibility also comes closer to effectively addressing white racism than does the idea of white guilt.

The idea of institutional racism refers to dimensions of constraint in nonwhite life that are held in place by customs and practices within institutions. These customs and practices are judged racist because of their present effects on nonwhites, not because of the feelings of those actively engaged in them or past injustices. The responsibility of whites in these contexts is to become aware of what they do individually to enact and support the racist customs and practices that are still taken for granted in American life. Still, there might be a residue of white unease with the way in which I seem to have analyzed white guilt away. I cannot address the psychological aspects of white guilt, because I am not a psychologist. However, white guilt seems to have an objective foundation, the existence of racial whiteness as an empirical fact, and that I am qualified to discuss.

THE IDEA OF WHITE RACIAL IDENTITY

I meant to evoke at the beginning of this chapter that I have found it embarrassing when whites assert that they are white in mixed company. I guess this is because it seems to be in bad taste, a lack of noblesse oblige, to assert that one belongs to an advantaged social category in the company of those who do not share that membership, especially when the person asserting whiteness has the appearance of someone who others would identify as white. In intellectual contexts, given what is now theoretically understood about race, the assertion that one is white evokes more serious problems than this.

The idea of white racial identity seems to refer to the fact that those who have it possess as a fact of physical heredity, membership in a distinct racial type. However, *race itself* does not exist biologically because there are no general genetic markers for it. It differs from sex, for example: From the presence of XX or XY, both primary and secondary sexual characteristics can be reliably predicted. The presence of XX and XY can be said to *cause* the presence, respectively, of ovaries and breasts, and testicles and upper-body strength. With race, there is nothing general that causes genes for light or dark skin hues, straight or curly hair growth, or any other physical trait associated with black, white, Asian, or Native American racial identity.

Whites are people who have no nonwhite ancestry. Blacks, Asians, and Indians are people who appear to conform to popular stereotypes of their groups or who have known ancestry of the relevant sort (these cultural determinants of race are what it means to say that race is socially constructed). In the United States, the difference between black and white has been socially enforced through the one drop rule. A person is black given a black ancestor anywhere in family descent. This "one drop of black blood" is of course a fiction—differences in the four major blood types do not conform to racial differences and have only a loose statistical connection with continental geography. Besides the lack of general biological racial characteristics, the different sets of traits associated with each race vary more within races than among races.

The social definitions of black and white are set up as contradictories of one another. White equals no black ancestors, and black equals at least one black ancestor. Two contradictory conditions cannot both obtain at the same time although one of them must. This means, and it has indeed been the case throughout much of American social history, that a person must be black or white, but not both and not neither. Such a stipulation is clearly rendered impossible in the same social reality that stipulates it, by the existence of individuals who are both black and white or neither black nor white. Mixed-race people satisfy the first condition, and both Asian Americans and Native Americans satisfy the second. The lack of fixed traits for each so-called race means that race cannot be inherited as is popularly thought. Rather, the specific physical characteristics variably associated with races in cultural contexts are inherited through family descent as is the rest of human biology. Race, therefore, supervenes on human genealogy or family inheritance. Those Americans who would, if pressed, base their whiteness on their families' whiteness are not relying on a biological concept of family descent but a social one. The instances of American families that have repudiated offspring of nonwhite inheritance, because they had nonwhite parents, are legion (and legendary).

It should go without saying that despite these scientific facts about the emptiness of biological race, race continues to loom as a switchboard for the allocation of cultural power. Once a person is plugged into her appropriate racial connection, the important—no, essential—mechanisms of social, emotional, economic, and political life are activated. So despite its unreality, racial identity remains a strong parameter of ordinary American life. Still it is important, given burgeoning contemporary ideas of white identity, to realize how empty those ideas are in terms of the kinds of biological facts to which people (mistakenly) think they refer. Not only is whiteness socially defined as a negation, which is in principle impossible to prove, but all racial categorizations lack empirical foundation.

If the white reader is still with me, there could be a question of what I think white people who do not want to be racist ought to do. I think that the individual obligations to not participate in institutional racism have not yet been seriously addressed by white scholars. I think that those who are categorized as white and are uncomfortable about the effects of that categorization might consider being not traitors to their race but defectors. I would be very interested in hearing from white liberatory antiracist scholars about what these suggestions mean to them and why they are or are not acceptable.

10

Despising an Identity
They Taught Me to Claim

Alison Bailey

> It is the nature of white privilege to find ever deeper places to hide.
> If the feminist attempt to deal with "difference" means simply the
> attempt to include the lives and concerns of some women without
> seriously challenging white middle-class privilege, then all the talk
> in the world about "difference" is simply dangerous. Tolerance is
> easy if those asked to express it needn't change a whit.
>
> —Elizabeth Spelman

$\mathcal{T}$he identity "white" woman feminist contains an ambiguity that arises
from my being simultaneously aware of both unearned race privilege and
sex/gender oppression. Historically, white women have had socially sanc-
tioned reasons for not noticing racism/white privilege. These include our
complex relationship to privilege made possible by racism, our associations
with and, for some, our dependence on white men, complicity in the
maintenance of institutionalized racism, and white guilt. In wrestling with
questions of racism/white privilege, I work toward being attentive to my
desire to control the conversation or to engage with issues of race in ways
that keep privilege invisible. Race privilege prevents me from noticing
what I strain so hard to keep before me. I try to face my initial reluctance
to engage in questions of privilege and at the same time not become so
absorbed in these questions that I fail to hear the voices of women of color.

White privilege takes on a new dimension for whites who resist common defensive or guilt-ridden responses to privilege (e.g., "I've worked
hard for everything I have," or "It's not my fault I was born into a system
that values whiteness," or "My ancestors never owned slaves") and struggle to understand the connections between our own ill-gotten advantages

and the genuine injustices that conspire to deny humanity to peoples of color. Exploring racism from a position of privilege initially left me angry, guilty, defensive, resistant, and sometimes feeling powerless in the face of what I perceived to be the impossible task of working to dismantle systems of domination to which I unknowingly contribute. When I first became aware of white privilege, I felt at once helpless and obligated to undo those injustices that appear to be undoable. From time to time I considered myself to be stuck in the unproductive place, to reverse Michelle Cliff's (1980) famous book title, of despising an identity they taught me to claim. White people who become aware of their privileges might be tempted to despise whiteness along with its accompanying privileges. It is this initial frustration with the perceived inescapability of white privilege that interests me.

To explore this inescapabilty, I want to recount a particular double bind I faced two years ago when I began, in a systematic (admittedly academic) way, to think through what it means to have white privilege, how white privilege is a product of racism, and whether there might be ways to use white privilege to undo racism. My project here is to explore a "dilemma of white privilege awareness" that leaves some privilege-cognizant whites trapped in the awkward position of knowing that it is both impossible to dispose of privilege and impossible to take advantage of it without perpetuating the systems of domination we wish to demolish. I explore both sides of the dilemma, marking detours, diversions, and natural sticking points (e.g., cultural impersonation, retreats to white ethnicity, and the temptation to shift discussions away from race to other oppressions) that prevent whites from engaging critically in discussions of racism. With the dilemma in place, I suggest two possible ways of avoiding this double bind: a conceptual solution and a pragmatic solution. In discussing the conceptual solution, I argue that the dilemma of privilege awareness is a false one that arises from an essentialist view of race. As a way of escaping the dilemma, I suggest a performative view of race based on Marilyn Frye's white/whitely distinction. Frye's solution helps undo the helplessness associated with the perceived inescapability of whiteness that gives rise to the dilemma, but it does little to move us toward questions of responsibility. A more pragmatic solution, one that moves us in the direction of responsibility, requires accepting as true the premise that privilege use reinscribes the value of privilege, while acknowledging that refusing to use privilege can amount to a waste of resources. I end the discussion by arguing that my efforts to find a way out of the dilemma of white privilege awareness do not focus on the right sort of questions. The best response to white privilege awareness should not be "How can I find a way out of this dilemma?" Rather, it should be "How do I begin thinking of privilege as a resource for undoing institutional racism?"

THE DILEMMA OF WHITE PRIVILEGE AWARENESS

> But it is seeming to me that race (together with racism and race privilege) is apparently *constructed as* something inescapable. And it makes sense that it would be, since such a construction would best serve those served by race and racism. *Of course* race and racism are impossible to escape; of course a white person is always in a sticky web of privilege that permits only acts which reinforce ("reinscribe") racism. This just means that some exit must be forced. That will require conceptual creativity, and perhaps conceptual violence. (Frye 1992a, 150)

Once I became aware of the privilege afforded to me by white racial classification, the question that came immediately to mind was, How ought I to act with respect to white privilege? This section is presented as a philosophical narrative on this question and summarizes how I've gradually come to understand privilege as a resource rather than as a dilemma.

My initial, admittedly unreflective response to white privilege was to explore ways of dissociating myself from whiteness and thus from the privileges that accompany it. If privilege is generated by injustice, I reasoned, I should consciously seek out ways of divesting myself of white privilege. After all, I didn't ask for these privileges; I was just born into a social/political system structured to benefit persons who appear to be white people. If these privileges are made possible by oppression, then I don't want them; I want to divest myself of them. But suppose divesting is impossible. Well, maybe there are responsible ways of using white privilege that do not perpetuate the institutionalized racism I want to demolish. Or, maybe all white privilege is by definition so toxic that it poisons everything with which it comes into contact. Or, perhaps there are varieties of white privilege I can use safely.

In working through these questions I found myself facing the dilemma Marilyn Frye hints at when she observes that race, racism, and race privilege are purposely "constructed as something inescapable" (1992a, 150–51). The inescapable character of white privilege initially presented itself to me in the form of a dilemma. On the one hand, to use Judith Levine's (1994) phrase, "privilege is written on my skin" (23). As a white woman I am stuck with privilege because I can't take off the invisible, weightless knapsack that grants me privilege.[1] On the other hand, if I am stuck with this knapsack, then I worry about whether its contents can be used safely. If this dilemma is real, I face a kind of political paralysis: I can't divest myself fully of privilege, and its use only fortifies the system I want to demolish. I can't lose it, and I don't want to use it. Where do I go from here?

The First Half of the Dilemma: Popular Strategies for Privilege Divestment

The first part of the dilemma works like this: when white privilege is extended to persons who appear white or act in ways we associate with whiteness, we understand white privilege as something that we cannot slough off, because one's appearance and racialized behaviors, dispositions, and habits are unconsciously embedded in her whole being. Whiteness is a source of privilege, so my interactions with individuals and institutions will be structured partly by the assumptions they make about my racial identity. I do not mean to imply that white privilege is an all-or-nothing phenomenon extended solely to people classified as white or to so-called nonwhites who can pass as white. Race privilege is mediated by sex/gender, class, sexual orientation, ability, ethnicity, and even one's politics. The strength of race privilege depends on how many other privileged conditions are present in my life, how long they have been present, and whether I am oppressed in ways that might weaken or mediate these privileges. Historically, whites have lost a degree of race privilege by marrying outside their race, associating with peoples of color, and engaging in civil rights and antiracist work.[2] Sometimes white privilege is extended to light-skinned Latinas/Latinos, African Americans, and people with multiracial identities who consciously or unconsciously pass as white. For example, in her autobiographical essay on passing, Adrian Piper explains (1996) how

> a benefit and a disadvantage of looking white is that most people treat you as though you were white. And so, because of how you've been treated, you come to expect this sort of treatment, not perhaps realizing that you're being treated this way because people think you are white, but rather falsely supposing that you're being treated this way because people think you are a valuable person. (260)

Those of us with white privilege rarely succeed in divesting from the unearned advantages that a white supremacist social order awards us. Privilege itself, as Frye (1992b) notes, is "an odd sort of self-regenerative thing which, once you've got it, cannot be simply shucked off like a too-warm jacket" (29). I cannot simply remove my knapsack when I become uncomfortable with the realization that the price at which my privilege, safety, comfort, or secure notion of the self is purchased is too high. If my very appearance and mannerisms act as magnets for special treatment, then I cannot easily arrange my life so as not to receive certain benefits and immunities. There appears to be no way to divest myself of privilege, but that does not mean some white people have not explored strategies for doing so.

Anger or discomfort with the costs of white privilege, white guilt, frustration with white intolerance, or just plain boredom with whiteness has led many whites down a bizarre path of racial disidentification. Cultural impersonation and unreflective detours to white ethnicity (or other oppressed identities) are two strategies whites use to avoid addressing racism/white privilege. When we recognize how members of our so-called "race" have colonized the globe, taken the natural resources of others as our own, and imposed our languages, customs, and values on members of so-called "nonwhite" peoples, it is tempting to want to dissociate ourselves from whiteness by either looking for the lost nonwhite ancestor or opting to "become Black" or "become Indian." I have searched my predominantly English, Irish, German, and Dutch heritage for Native American or African ancestors in hopes of discovering at least some non-European blood that would make me "less white." In retrospect, this exercise was motivated more by guilt and my desire to dilute privilege than by a genuine interest in my heritage or social change.

Other attempts at privilege divestment have led whites to impersonate or adopt the customs or cultures of peoples that are unrelated to their own heritage. A young pastor working in the South Side of Chicago in the mid-1960s, for example, tells the story of how the more he learned about racism, the guiltier he felt about being white. He came to hate being white and to feel alienated from white society. To cope with this discomfort, he tried to shed his white identity by trying to act, walk, talk, and even think as if he were Black. His performance ended when a Black friend made him stand in front of a mirror and gently reintroduced him to himself as a white person. It was only after this incident that the pastor learned that if he were going to deal with racism, he was going to have to learn to love himself (Barndt and Ruehle 1988).

Cultural impersonation does not divest whites of privilege; as the story illustrates, it makes us look silly. In most cases, "acting Black" so as to avoid confronting whiteness is both a trivialization of oppression faced by African Americans and a disingenuous destruction of one's own identity.[3] These performances reinforce the self-hatred one may feel as a result of white privilege awareness. Likewise, claims such as "I really feel like a Black person inside," "I just know I have a Mexicano soul trapped inside an Anglo body," or "I'm sure I was Shawnee in a former life" allow the speaker to avoid privilege altogether by imaginatively refashioning her or his identity as privilege-free. Andrea Smith (1992), a Cherokee woman, explains her frustration with white New Age feminists who emulate indigenous spiritual practices as a way to dissociate themselves from whiteness.

> The trivialization of oppression is compounded by the fact that nowadays anyone can be Indian if she or he chooses. All that is required is that one be Indian in a former life, or take part in a sweat lodge, or be mentored by a "medicine woman," or read a how-to book. [If theoretically] anyone can be an "Indian," then the term no longer refers to those who have survived 500 years of colonization and genocide. . . . When everyone becomes "Indian," then it is easy to lose sight of the specificity of oppression faced by those who are Indian in *this* life. (44–45)

To reinvent oneself as Black or Navajo without having experienced the hardships faced by these groups misses the point of doing antiracism work. As a friend of mine who works with the Sumo people in Nicaragua once told me, "If you want to be Indian, try getting rid of everything you own except for what you are wearing, and don't eat for three days." Yet, in making this claim I do not mean to deny the possibility or importance of discovering a particular racial or ethnic identity that one's family has kept hidden for any number of reasons, such as the desire to pass. Reinventing oneself as Black or as an indigenous person because one does not want to deal with discomfort is not the same as having to reconsider one's identity as a result of unearthing a missing piece of one's family heritage.

It might be objected that often people of color have passed for white, and if they can pass, then whites should be able to do the same. For whites to pass as Black, Kickapoo, or Latina/Latino is not the political equivalent of African Americans, Mexicanos, mixed-race, or indigenous peoples "passing" for white. Passing in both directions requires a degree of inauthenticity, but unlike African Americans who sometimes had to make the difficult choice to pass as white for reasons of economic survival, cultural impersonation by whites is an exercise in privilege. White appropriation of the "romantic" qualities ascribed to the Lakota-Sioux or African Americans is made possible by the fact that white identity retains its social value despite decisions to fiddle with it.[4] In her analysis of John Howard Griffin's experiment in racial cross-dressing, Gayle Wald (1996) observes that whites in general, and white men in particular, traditionally have always had greater freedom to play with their identities at no permanent cost to themselves. The white "sanction to 'pass' inevitably hinges on the structure of race itself, that is, on a system in which some racial identifications are more rigidly organized and maintained than others." Griffin's experiment takes this liberty for granted in a way that the case of Blacks passing as white does not; his "passing ensues from a sovereignty over identity rather than from the exigencies of economic necessity or personal safety" (Wald 1996, 162).

Contrast Griffin's experiment, or the slightly different case of the white/Anglo New Age feminist who convinces herself that she was Indian in a former life, with cases of peoples of color who "pass" for reasons of personal safety, economic necessity, or to escape the genuine hardships that come with membership in historically disenfranchised groups. As most narratives by persons of color passing as white reveal, the economic benefits of passing rarely outweigh the emotional costs. Passing as white reached an all time peak between 1880 and 1925, when Jim Crow became so oppressive that many light-skinned African Americans and multiracial persons passed to escape the racial barriers to employment opportunities, to avoid the humiliation and inconvenience of segregation codes, or to escape police hassles directed at nonwhites (Davis 1991). Yet even during these peak years, the vast majority did not pass on a permanent basis. The pain of separation from community, tribe, and family, condemnation from members of one's community, fear of being discovered by whites, and the loss of the security of one's community are reasons why many who could pass often choose not to.

If cultural impersonation is nothing more than an exercise in privilege that makes most whites look foolish, perhaps less ridiculous strategies for divestment exist. Often awareness of white privilege is met with detours to ethnicity (e.g., "Yeah, but I'm not like *those* whites—I come from a family of Italian immigrants," or "I'm not white; I'm Irish Catholic," or "My ancestors came from England, but as indentured servants"). There is a hierarchy of privilege within white communities that favors Anglo-Saxon Protestants over Italians, Jews, Poles, Irish, Catholics, or Spanish speakers, and embracing one's heritage in this way is certainly not equivalent to embracing romanticized identities that are a reflection of my tastes or interests and not of my ancestry or cultural heritage. But these moves are tricky: depending on the approach, self-reflection on one's ethnicity, sexuality, or class can be either an important resource for white antiracist work or a deliberate detour from confronting white racism. I do not deny that an examination of how complex systems of domination (e.g., racism, heterosexism, anti-Semitism, sexism, ablism) are interrelated is essential to any conversation on oppression. My worry is that whites sometimes deliberately shift the conversation from racism/privilege to discussions of ethnicity, anti-Semitism, heterosexism, or ablism as a way to avoid confronting racism.

These diversions to other oppressed identities shift the spotlight from white privilege/racism to stories of one's own hardship. When discussions of white ethnicity don't engage history and politics, they are useless in the service of antiracism. If, for example, in exploring my German roots I ignore that fact that in spite of harsh treatment by Anglo-Saxons upon immigration, Germans worked hard and were eventually treated with dignity and respect, whereas persons of African descent who worked hard yet still, in many cases, are not extended dignity and respect, then my discussion of ethnicity fails to address the role of racism in the formation of German American identity. However, not all explorations of white ethnicity are without merit, and understanding my history can be integral to a critical comprehension of the ways in which the history of race relations is reenacted in daily encounters. Unpacking white privilege requires that I critically explore family and community histories as a way of understanding the historical formation of racial dynamics, why whiteness has been equated with culturelessness, and how oppression is not limited to peoples of color. Most materials and workshops on antiracism directed toward whites emphasize the importance of rediscovering one's ethnic heritage or recovering uncounted acts of resistance to racism by white people (e.g., John Brown's abolitionist movement, Quaker resistance, the writings of Lillian Smith and Anne Braden, or Sarah Jane Foster's dedication to teaching freedmen) as ways of beginning to construct what some have identified as a "new white consciousness" or European American antiracist identity.[5]

Dismantling racism requires looking critically at the connections between the purposeful construction of white identity and institutionalized racism. When selfishness and escapism are at work, I lose sight of my reasons for examining white privilege and become satisfied with any gesture of transformation that allows me to think of myself as a "good white person." Detours from white privilege do not remove me from the system of privilege; they relocate me within it by reasserting my needs at the center of the analysis. It appears infinitely easier to refashion my identity as "non-white," as "ethnic white," or as "oppressed as a woman" than it is to struggle to understand how I benefit from racism. These defensive moves are, to use Ruth Frankenberg's (1993) phrase, "power-evasive repertoires" designed to alleviate the white guilt, pain, and self-hatred that almost always accompany privilege awareness (141–57). Strategies for divestment from privilege not only fail to rid whites of privilege; they fail as strategies for antiracist work because they shift our focus away from injustice.

The Second Half of the Dilemma: Is It Possible to Use Privilege in Ways That Do Not Reinforce Racism?

That escapist divestment strategies fail to release me of privilege might be taken as evidence that white privilege is inescapable under current social and political conditions.[6] If the obsession with getting rid of privilege is misguided and politically useless, perhaps a better approach is to explore the possibilities of using white privilege in ways that do not perpetuate structural inequalities. Perhaps I can open my knapsack and use the tools white privilege affords me to assist oppressed groups in overcoming the everyday racial barriers placed in their paths. Suppose I, a white professor, have gone to the Financial Aid Office with Nina, an African American student who has just been notified that she has received a full scholarship for the school year. She is registered for classes and has paid her fees, but her name does not appear in the registrar's database; the staff assume she has dropped out but has come by to get her check. They inform her that they cannot give her the check until her name appears in the database, because they have had problems with "students from Chicago, like her," who pick up checks and then drop out of school. I accompany Nina to the office, and I speak on her behalf, demand to speak to administrators in the registrar's office, and make everybody in the office give Nina the appropriate attention and treat her like a deserving scholarship recipient. Here, because my voice is heard by the staff in a way that Nina's is not, I am using my privilege in a way that we both hope will help her get the money she needs to pay her fall tuition. Eventually, her check is released. If this act is helpful to Nina, what might it mean to say that exercising privilege reinforces institutionalized racism?

My playing the white faculty card—intervening on behalf of Nina—does not give the staff in the Financial Aid Office a lesson in how to treat students of color in a way that is not rude, neglectful, or suspicious. They will still be suspicious of Black students and treat them with caution, and they will still be accommodating to most white faculty and students. My performance gives the staff another opportunity to practice being accommodating to people with the right color, accent, mannerisms, and job title in the accepted way. After I vouch for Nina, she receives the attention she deserves. But the whole performance reinscribes, rather than undermines, the script that teaches the staff to listen to and believe white people and does not honor the explanations of most students of color. I've helped Nina negotiate her way around barriers that would have taken more time and energy if she had to negotiate them on her own. I've helped her gain mobility in a system that distrusts African American students, but I've done nothing to facilitate movement for the next scholarship recipient. By locating racism in the biased actions of the staff at one campus office, I've treated racism as a problem of attitude and not structure. In the end my actions are resistant to racism but they have not challenged the system of structural inequalities. My intervention not only reinforces recognition of racial privilege but also masks the racist stereotypes and suppositions held by the Financial Aid Office staff.

It is unclear that every instance of playing the white card works in this way, and I don't wish to suggest that we can generalize from this example. In using this illustration, my point is to make a strong case for the binding nature of the dilemma by providing an example of how privilege use reinscribes the system that grants privilege. The example illustrates Audre Lorde's (1984) often cited claim that we cannot "use the master's tools to dismantle the master's house." In the case of Nina, to paraphrase Lorde, I have "temporarily beat the master at his own game, but I've not brought about any genuine change" (112). If there appear to be no ways to play the white card safely, then must I consciously avoid using privilege in order to discontinue reinforcing racist values?

This example is vulnerable to a variety of criticisms, and I return to these in the final section. At present it is enough to note how a double bind results from the prima facie inescapability of white privilege. There is no way to suddenly stop having privilege, and there is no way to use privilege without reinforcing the system that gives it value. If the claims I have sketched out on both sides of the dilemma are true, then I am trapped: I can neither fully divest myself of white privilege, nor can I use privilege without reinforcing the structure of the very systems I wish to demolish. Privilege is impossible to dispose of safely and too toxic to use. What should I do?

CONCEPTUAL CREATIVITY
AS A WAY OUT OF THE DILEMMA

> Those progressive white intellectuals who are particularly critical of "essentialist" notions of identity when writing about mass culture, race and gender have not focused their critiques on white identity and the way essentialism informs representations of whiteness. It is always the nonwhite, or in some cases the nonheterosexual Other, who is guilty of essentialism. (hooks 1992, 30)

I reflect on the dilemma before me. I wonder whether I am making any assumptions about race or whiteness that cause me to think of privilege as something unshakable, to be escaped. I wonder whether there are ways in which my own white identity might shape the way I address this issue. It occurs to me that it is possible to be aware of race privilege without being critical of the extent to which the construction of privilege depends on essentialist views of race, and this seems to be my predicament. In my mind I know that "white" and "whiteness" do not refer to essential properties of white people but to persons designated as white as the result of political and historical processes. But I still seem to slip into thinking that this designation is somehow unshakable. I am "race-cognizant," aware of the role white privilege plays in institutionalized racism, yet I unconsciously continue to think of races as historically fixed kinds. It is this essentialist hangover that creates the dilemma at hand. The view that a person's racial identity is a given, "natural," unchangeable historical fact is an integral part of complex systems of domination that generate race-based privileges. Essentialist systems of classification, biological, political, or otherwise, do not tolerate ambiguity. Discriminatory practices such as racial segregation, redlining, and "color taxes" only work if there are strict rules for racial classification. Refusal to serve African Americans at a lunch counter is only possible if we have a system in place that can, with some accuracy, pick out who is and who is not Black. Extending privilege to whites is only possible if one has a rough idea of who counts as white. If I embrace the idea that being white is an unchangeable fact about my identity, and if white privilege is made possible by this system, then questions about how white people should act with regard to privilege can only be cast in terms of a choice between finding ways to use privilege safely or divesting from privilege. If racial identities are constructed within social contexts for political purposes, then we need to find ways of reshaping racial identity in more liberatory directions. Forcing an exit from the dilemma means replacing essentialist views of race with views that construct racial identities as ambiguous, open-ended, fluid products of the interplay between a social group's history, social conditioning, and the chosen behavior of individual persons.

Recognizing this essentialist stumbling block, Marilyn Frye (1992a) makes the case for language that allows us to think clearly about whiteness in ways that are not essentially connected to color but that are related to color in some way. Paralleling the distinction feminists make between *maleness*, something persons are born with by virtue of their biological sex, and *masculinity,* something that is socially connected to maleness but is largely the result of social training, Frye argues that we need a set of terms in racial discourse that capture the equivalent of what masculinity expresses in discourses on gender/sex. She coins "whitely" and "whiteliness" as the racial equivalents of masculine and masculinity, respectively. "Being whiteskinned (like being male) is a matter of physical traits presumed to be physically determined: being whitely (like being masculine) [is] conceive[d] as a deeply ingrained way of being in the world" (1992a, 150–51). The connection between whiteliness and light-complected skin is contingent, so it is possible for persons who are not members of the social group "white" to perform in whitely ways, and for persons who are white not to perform in whitely ways.

I find it helpful to think of these "ways of being," (e.g., performed attitudes and behaviors) as scripts. Like sexism, racism is a social/political system of domination that comes with expected performances, attitudes, and behaviors, which reinforce and reinscribe unjust hierarchies.[7] Feminists have long been attentive to the ways in which gender roles encourage habits and nurture systems that value men's ideas, activities, and achievements over those of women. Just as gender roles reinforce patriarchy, so might whitely performances, or scripts, reinforce systems that value white experiences and achievements over the experiences and achievements of peoples of color. As systems of domination, the existence of racism and sexism require everyone's daily consensus and collaboration. To understand the nature of this collaboration, it is helpful to think of the attitudes and behaviors expected of one's particular racial group as performances that follow historically preestablished *scripts.* Scripts differ with a subject's location within systems of domination. What all racial scripts in the United States of (North) America have in common, however, is that all people learn, and are more or less expected, to follow scripts that sustain dominant group privileges. Judith Butler's (1990) analysis of gender as "performatively constructed" is easily extended to racial scripts. Like gender, race may, in part, be thought of in terms of "the repeated stylization of the body, a set of repeated acts within a highly rigid regulatory frame that congeal over time to produce the appearance of substance, of a natural sort of being" (33). When the concept of racial scripts is applied locally, what it means to be a white woman in rural Kentucky, an African American man living in urban Chicago, or a Puertoriqueño is extended to include a person's gestures, dialect, attitudes, conception of personal space, gut reactions to certain phenomena, and bodily awareness. Attention to race as performative (scripted) reveals the less visible structural regulatory function of racial scripts.

To get a picture of what whiteliness is, Frye (1992a) sifts through narrative essays written by African Americans for descriptions of how whites appear through their eyes. In a "free and speculative way" she uses these narratives to piece together an account of whitely ways of being in the world. As a child, the whitely script Frye learned to animate taught her that white people know right from wrong and had the responsibility to see that right was done. Being white/whitely means having an undying faith in the goodness of other whites and in one's own rightness and propriety. According to the whitely view, whites have a firm belief in their authority and expertise on practical matters and make it clear to people of other races that our authority and expertise are not to be challenged. Whites are just, goodwilled, honest, fair, and ethical. Nobody admits to being prejudiced; our work ethic tells us that everyone has worked hard for all they have; we always vote for and hire the most qualified candidate regardless of their race, ethnicity, sex, or religion. White people are rule governed and punctual (Frye 1992a, 154–57). The majority of whitely scripts also have a strong corporeal element that emerges in bodily behaviors, gestures, and reactions to persons whom we think of as being unlike ourselves. Everyone is on some level attentive to the race of persons with whom they interact, and this shapes our encounters. Fear and avoidance of people of color and the spaces they inhabit is a strong component of whitely scripts. African Americans are commonly on the receiving end of these avoidance behaviors, expressions of nervousness, and stereotyping that make them feel noticed or marked.[8] These scripts are deeply ingrained, and their repeated animation reinscribes a racial order in which white lives, culture, and experiences are valued over and at the expense of the lives of persons of color who occupy fearful bodies and are cast as deviant, dirty, criminal, ugly, or degenerate.

Adding an account of scripts to Frye's constructivist view of race offers an alternative to essentialist constructions. When the question "How do I stop having white privilege?" is replaced with the question "Is it possible to willfully stop animating whitely scripts?" the dilemma dissolves. I cannot, in most cases, prevent others from extending privilege to me because I am perceived as white. I can, however, examine my behaviors and attitudes and eliminate the ones that promote white supremacy. Thinking in terms of scripts has liberatory potential; scripts after all can be broken, rewritten, or played subversively out of context. I do think it is possible for white people to stop animating the whitely scripts that teach us to believe in our authority and expertise, to be controlling, or to distrust and fear people of color and replace them with habits that do not reinforce racial hierarchies.

To refuse compliance to racist and white supremacist scripts allows an exit from the dilemma and may even alleviate feelings of helplessness on the part of those with unjustified privileges. However, this tidy conceptual solution does not address my initial question of how ought I to *act* with regard to white privilege once I become aware of it. I hope to begin to answer this question by attending to the fact that privilege can be a resource.

PRIVILEGE AS A RESOURCE?

In her essay "Ethics of Method: Greasing the Machine and Telling Stories," Joyce Trebilcot (1991, 46) asks what motivates feminists to choose some philosophical topics and approaches over others. I have a similar concern: I wonder why I initially chose to see privilege as a dilemma rather than as a resource. Why was my first response to the question "What do I do with privilege now that I am aware of it?" either to find ways to divest myself of privilege or to find ways of using privilege that don't reinscribe the complex systems of domination I want to eliminate? Why was it that I first understood privilege as toxic, as a dilemma to be overcome? The idea that white privilege is poisonous or problematic is, no doubt, laughable from the standpoint of peoples of color. White antiracist explorations of privilege must involve more than orchestrating conceptual end runs around racial essentialism for the sake of easing discomfort. Framing questions of privilege in terms of a dilemma that needs to be solved keeps the conversation focused on me. From the point of view of activists dedicated to coalition building across differences the dilemma is self-regarding: in the end all it really amounts to is a more philosophically sophisticated way of wrestling with white guilt. It does not allow me to move in the direction of creative political action.

Recall that my project here is to examine white privilege in ways that are both critical of privilege and race and that engage with racial differences honestly. If I hope to "escape the dilemma," I lose sight of the daily battles and concerns of peoples of color. African Americans, Asian Americans, Arapahos, or Latinas/Latinos are not concerned with whether white people can find philosophically sound ways out of their dilemmas; they want to know whether I can be counted on as an ally, whether I am willing to take risks, whether I am listening to them, and whether I am willing to use privilege to help gain access to resources and opportunities in a system designed to exclude them. Philosophical focus on my own dilemma does not engage directly with these concerns. More pragmatic responses need to be explored.

One pragmatic response to the dilemma of white privilege awareness is to refuse to engage it on the grounds that a self-regarding focus diverts attention from more immediate political issues. Suppose I began my inquiry into white privilege/racism with the understanding that under current social arrangements, use of privilege always perpetuates the racist systems that give it currency. If the institutionalized racism that keeps privilege in its place will not be dismantled anytime in the near future, it makes sense to think of privilege as a potential resource rather than as an obstacle. Although the master's tools may not be able to successfully dismantle the master's house, they may be just the tools we need to gain access to its contents. Since these tools gain their strength only within a system that privileges whites, they can never be used *safely*, but they may be used *effectively*. Furthermore, refusal to use the tools privilege affords us to break into the master's house may amount to protecting the house. In a letter to *The Gay Community News*, Audre Lorde (1990) explains:

> Privilege is not criminal. Acquiring it by exploitation is abuse—as is non-use of privilege. . . . The most problematic reason class is so difficult to discuss in Lesbian and Gay communities is because those of us who have benefited from class privilege or white-skin privilege are often reluctant to look at [it]. . . lest we find ourselves morally or socially obligated to give them up or share them. We are therefore also reluctant to use those benefits and privileges in the service of what we believe needs being done, because to use privilege requires admitting to privilege, requires moving beyond guilt and accusation into creative

action. And, of course, unused privilege becomes a weapon in the hand of our enemies, and we wind up being used against our lovers, our friends, other members of our communities. Privilege, like power, is relative. (27)

So how might it be possible to see privilege as something to both use and give up?

This passage from Lorde's letter suggests that privilege in and of itself is not inherently evil, harmful, or criminal; like power and strength, privilege can be abused when it is used to attain ends that are harmful to others. Keeping both the lessons of the dilemma and Lorde's observations before us, it makes sense to say that it is impossible to give up privilege in the sense that it cannot be abandoned completely. What must be given up, then, is not privilege per se, but *harmful* uses of privilege. To use privilege as a resource for antiracist activities is to give up its abusive power. In this way we can consistently think of privilege as something that is both used and given up. Learning to think of privilege as a resource or political tool, rather than as a paralyzing dilemma, perhaps will increase the chances of privilege-cognizant whites organizing around issues of institutional racism. My refusal to use the master's tools because I understand their very use as an action that reinscribes privilege in ways that perpetuate systems of oppression can be a self-regarding reason for withholding resources marginalized racial groups need *now*!

The earlier example of helping Nina through the red tape at the Financial Aid Office purposely focuses on a specific instance in which one person is faced with the problem of how to use privilege safely. What if I just tried to use this resource effectively? My example is vulnerable to a variety of criticisms. First, some might object that my discussion of privilege in the context of the Financial Aid Office keeps my white angst, and not Nina's anger and frustration, at the center of discussion. But I don't know of a way to have this discussion without naming my responsibility. Insofar as it is possible for me to anticipate Nina's reply, I imagine that she might see a white person's refusal to use privilege on the grounds that it can't be used safely as a selfish response to injustice—a refusal to act on her behalf. If I decide not to use privilege for fear of buttressing the system that gives privilege currency, then I get to decide what aspects of oppression get addressed. My decision is based not on Nina's needs but on my comfort. I want to concentrate my energies on macroinequalities—long-term structural change—rather than on the immediate needs of those in positions of powerlessness. Quick fixes do little to empower Nina and may be read as patronizing exercises in noblesse oblige. My actions might even mark her as "a problem student" in the eyes of the administration. None of these criticisms count as sound reasons for refusing to use privilege, but they are important to take into account when considering creative approaches to using privilege. For example, it is probably not enough for me to just march into the office and fix things. Using privilege as resource requires that Nina and I sit down together and find ways of calling attention to the racist suppositions of the administrators in ways that foreground her interests and her perspective.

Why has it taken me so long to see privilege as a potential resource? It's one thing to make white privilege visible. It's quite another to make oneself accountable for privilege by choosing to collectively explore strategies for redistributing resources, especially when these strategies require placing myself in an uncomfortable or vulnerable position. As Lorde observes, those who benefit from race and class privilege are often reluctant to look at it because on some level we fear we may find ourselves morally or socially obligated to give up our unearned advantages or share these benefits. But with awareness comes responsibility. The dilemma of white privilege awareness has the virtue of making privilege visible, but it does little to move us toward taking responsibility for privilege. The call to examine whiteness sparked by the dilemma is not a call to renounce privilege or to embrace passivity by avoiding responsibility for it. Since privilege is not something that can be sloughed off like a too warm jacket, and since despising the identity they taught me to claim is an unproductive response to privilege, whites genuinely committed to antiracist work can, for the time being, best use social privilege and power to promote social change.

ENDNOTES

This piece is dedicated to the memory of Linda Wiener Morris, whose generous spirit, sharp wit, and years of sound advice will remain with me always. I would also like to thank Lisa Heldke, Sarah Hoagland, Amber Katherine, María Lugones, Peg O'Connor, and Nancy Tuana for their helpful comments and conversations that helped shape this piece. I would also like to thank Joan Olsson, whose workshops allowed me to begin thinking about privilege in political ways. I presented an earlier version of this essay titled "The Paradox of White Privilege Awareness" at the National Endowment for the Humanities "Feminist Epistemologies," Summer Seminar, University of Oregon, Eugene, 1996.

1. The metaphor of the invisible knapsack comes from Peggy McIntosh (1991), who describes white privilege as "an invisible package of unearned assets that I can count on cashing in each day, but about which I was meant to remain oblivious" (71). Privileges in this sense include the following: I can if I wish arrange to be in the company of people of my race most of the time; I am never asked to speak for all the people of my racial group; I can dress anyway I want and not have my appearance explained by the perceived tastes of my race and, whether I use checks, credit cards, or cash I can be fairly sure that my skin color will not count against the appearance of my financial reliability. In most instances I can be assured of having the public trust.

2. The label "race traitor" is one way of marking whites who engage in these sorts of activities. Two examples come to mind. John Howard Griffin, who in his ethnojournalistic experiment of passing as a Black man in the south in the early 1960s, wrote a series of articles in *Sepia* magazine and later the book *Black Like Me* (1976), exposing white southern racism in a way it had not been exposed before. This disclosure was met by some with anger and hostility. He was branded a race traitor in his hometown of Mansfield, Texas, and a mannequin painted half black and half white, with a yellow stripe down its back, was burned in effigy. Traitorous acts have also been meet with legal repercussions. For example, in *The Wall Between,* Anne Braden (1958) describes how when she and her husband Carl sold their home in Louisville, Kentucky, to a Black man named Andrew Wade in 1954, they were indicted for sedition—attempting to overthrow the government of Kentucky.

3. This claim is problematic. There are instances of mixed-race and "white" children who grow up in black neighborhoods who speak African American dialects and "act black." I don't mean to say that these children eschew whiteness; given their cultural context, their performances do not count as impersonation. My comments about inauthenticity are directed at whites who may "act black" or "act Chicana/Chicano" for the sake of distancing themselves from whiteness.

4. I recognize there may be another dimension to impersonation here. Impersonation in and of itself may not be bad. The theatricality of racial impersonation may also be a way of fiddling with identity in the ways similar to the ways in which drag fiddles with gender. Simply fiddling with gender or race, however, is not enough. One needs to play with it in ways that are critical of these categories. Cross-dressing won't help us dismantle sexism, and cross-racial passing won't dismantle racism, but these might still be useful activities if paired with critical analyses of gender or race that makes visible uses and misuses of these categories.

5. See, for example, the workshops given by The People's Institute for Survival, New Orleans, Louisiana; Joan Olsson's "Cultural Bridges," Hamburg, Pennsylvania. See also "Rediscovering a Heritage Lost," by Joseph Barndt and Charles Ruehle, available in a special edition of *Sojourners* (1988): 73–78, through the Sojourner's Resource Center, P.O. Box 29272, Washington, D.C., 20017, or by calling (202) 636-3637.

6. It is important to emphasize that just because I cannot divest myself of white privilege under the current sociopolitical system of racial order, it does not follow that white privilege is unshakable. That absolutely nothing I do can take away my whiteness is false; I can make choices. The history of racial formation in the United States illustrates that races have never been static. As Mab Segrest (1994) explains, "If we white folks were constructed by history, we can, over time and as a people, unconstruct ourselves. . . . How then, to move masses of white people to become traitors to the concept of race?" (195). If white privilege is a learned invention, then it can be unlearned. If racial categories change, perhaps experimentation with reinventing new white identities is a move toward undoing the racial order that gives whiteness its currency. One of the presuppositions that holds the dilemma of white privilege awareness in place, as I will argue, is the idea that our existing racial order is a permanent human condition.

7. For a more detailed account of whitely scripts see my "Locating Traitorous Identities: Toward a View of Privilege-Cognizant White Character," *Hypatia* 13, no. 3 (Summer 1998): 27–42.

8. On this point see Iris Young's (1990, 130–36) summary of Anthony Gidden's work on discursive and practical consciousness in *Justice and the Politics of Difference*.

WORKS CITED

Barndt, Joseph, and Charles Ruehle. 1988. "Rediscovering a Heritage Lost:" A European-American Anti-Racist Identity." In *America's Original Sin: A Study Guide on White Racism*. Special edition of *Sojourners*. Washington, D.C.: Sojourner's Resource Center.

Braden, Anne. 1958. *The Wall Between*. New York: Monthly Review Press.

Butler, Judith. 1990. *Gender Trouble: Feminism and the Subversion of Identity*. New York: Routledge.

Cliff, Michelle. 1980. *Claiming an Identity They Taught Me to Despise*. Watertown, Mass.: Persephone.

Davis, F. James. 1991. *Who Is Black? One Nation's Definition*. University Park, Penn.: Pennsylvania University Press.

Frankenburg, Ruth. 1993. *White Women, Race Matters: The Social Construction of Whiteness*. Minneapolis: University of Minnesota Press.

Frye, Marilyn. 1992a. "White Woman Feminist." In *Willful Virgin: Essays in Feminism*. Freedom, Calif.: Crossing.

———. 1992b. "Who Wants a Piece of the Pie?" In *Willful Virgin: Essays in Feminism*. Freedom, Calif.: Crossing.

Griffin, John Howard. 1976. *Black Like Me*. Boston: Signet.

hooks, bell. 1992. *Black Looks: Race and Representation.* Boston: South End.

Levine, Judith. 1994. "White Like Me." *Ms.* 4, no. 5 (March/April): 22–24.

Lorde, Audre. 1984. *Sister Outsider.* Freedom, Calif.: Crossing Press.

———. 1990. "Unused Privilege Is a Weapon in the Hand of Our Enemies." *Gay Community News* 17, no. 27 (January 21–27): 3.

McIntosh, Peggy. 1991. "White Privilege and Male Privilege: A Personal Account of Coming to See Correspondences through Work in Women's Studies." In *Race, Class and Gender: An Anthology*, ed. Margaret L. Andersen and Patricia Hill Collins. New York: Wadsworth. First published as Working Paper No. 189. Wellesley, Mass.: Center for Research of Women, Wellesley College.

Piper, Adrian. 1996. "Passing for White, Passing for Black." In *Passing and the Fictions of Identity*, ed. Elaine K. Ginsberg. Durham, N.C.: Duke University Press.

Reilly, Wayne E., ed. 1990. *Sarah Jane Foster: Teacher of the Freedmen: A Diary and Letters.* Charlottesville: University Press of Virginia.

Segrest, Mab. 1994. *Memoir of a Race Traitor.* Boston: South End.

Smith, Andrea. 1992. "For Those Who Were Indian in a Former Life." *Ms.* 2, no. 3 (November/December): 44–45.

Smith, Lillian. 1949. *Killers of the Dream.* New York: Norton.

Spelman, Elizabeth V. 1988. *The Inessential Woman: Problems of Exclusion in Feminist Thought.* Boston: Beacon.

Trebilcot, Joyce. 1991. "Ethics of Method: Greasing the Machine and Telling Stories." *Feminist Ethics*, ed. Claudia Card. Lawrence: University of Kansas Press.

Wald, Gayle. 1996. "'A Most Disagreeable Mirror': Reflections on White Identity in *Black Like Me*." In *Passing and the Fictions of Identity*, ed. Elaine K. Ginsberg. Durham, N.C.: Duke University Press.

Young, Iris Marion. 1990. *Justice and the Politics of Difference.* Princeton, N.J.: Princeton University Press.

11

The Other Colors of Whiteness:
A Travelogue

Lisa Tessman and Bat-Ami Bar On

We—Ami, an expatriate immigrant from Israel to the United States, and Lisa, born and raised in the United States—are on an extended visit to Israel where we are immersed in a racial/ethnic system different from that of the United States. The two countries' configurations of ethnicity/race as well as our relationships to each country, as original home, adopted home, or supposed "homeland," shape these reflections on the significance of whiteness. We are both Jewish—in the quite different ways that a Sabra (native-born Israeli Jew) and an American can be Jewish—and in the United States we are both white. But as it turns out, it is also in our whiteness that we are so very different from each other.

Ami: On this visit to Israel I am quickly reminded in subtle and unsubtle ways that, contrary to the United States, here color is not the most important marker of racial or ethnic distinctions and, hence, not the most useful marker for ethnically or racially based discrimination. Being white here, while signaling Jewish-European ancestry (generally referred to as *Ashkenazi* ancestry), counts socially only if one is from the right European countries and during the right time—for example, at present a new immigrant from Russia.[1]

What marks one more than color here are things that signal not distance from blackness but rather a national kind of distance from the local, from the cultures of Southwest Asia (the Middle East), North Africa, and the cultures of the Balkans. In short, what matters is distance from Arab and strongly Arab-influenced cultures, including even cultures where some form of Arab rule, specifically that of Turkey, continued into the nineteenth and early twentieth centuries. Not that this distance did not have in the past an East European flavor and now has a West European/North American flavor, insofar as it is the proximity to them rather than to Southeast Asia, the rest of Africa, or South America that is considered better. This flavoring, especially its more current versions, has not yet fully colored ethnic/racial distinctions.[2]

Lisa: I think that as Jewish Israeli and American Jew you and I see through eyes trained by systems with different constructions of us/them. The us/them division that I learned growing up is white/black. Since I was raised quite assimilated, it is a stretch for me to think of the central division as Jew/Gentile, and even then, Gentile tends to mean Christian rather than Muslim. But from here in Israel, as I reflect on the patterns of racial formation in the United States[3]—the patterns familiar to me—they appear strange. This is something I realize upon shifting imaginatively into the local, unfamiliar framework: us/them is primarily national and is thus Jewish/Arab. The visuals of this binary do not work for me: I cannot, unless they are marked by traditional dress or sometimes language (an unreliable marker since some Jews speak Arabic and many Palestinians speak Hebrew), distinguish Jews from Arabs, and "black" still cues "difference" to me though they are Jewish and hence "us" rather than "them."

I have frequent encounters with this startling shift into the local binary. In one such incident we are at the Central Bus Station in Tel Aviv, where a few Israeli Defense Force (IDF) soldiers mill around waiting to board buses. Unaccustomed to the sight, my eyes are always drawn to their assault rifles, carried so naturally that they appear to be part of their clothing. Their uniformed presence is supposed to make me feel protected against the enemy, and if I look down at the photograph on the front page of the newspaper I am carrying, I see exactly that: IDF soldiers aiming their weapons at Palestinians in Hebron. "We" are firing rubber bullets and "they" are throwing stones; two of "us" and fifteen of "them" were wounded yesterday. In the bus station the uniforms and rifles tell me that I am to think of these young women and men as "us," but as I look at one, an Ethiopian Jew whom I would have called "black" in the States, I recall a phrase that a white student of mine used as she described first encountering blacks. She had been puzzled, at about age six, when witnessing her parents' friendliness to a black acquaintance, and wondered to herself, "But aren't we at war with them?" She had apparently gathered an awareness that whites in the United States are indeed engaged in a warlike destruction of black lives.

I shift back: "we" (namely whites, which includes at least those Jews who are Ashkenazi and assimilated enough) are not at war with "them" (blacks, which must include this Ethiopian Jew, as skin color tells me within a U.S. racial framework), but rather "we" (Jews of any skin color and any ethnicity or background, and here in Israel, the majority of Jews are shades of lightish brown) are united against an Arab other who, like the Jews, would officially be white within the U.S. racial framework.[4]

Nevertheless, while supposedly united in this nationalist project here in Israel, the Jewish "we" is also hierarchically divided in some ways that mirror U.S. racism and in other ways that diverge from it. For instance, Ethiopian Jews seem to both count and not count as black and to experience a racism both similar to and different from what blacks in the U.S. experience. A (*Sabra, Mizrachi,* lesbian) friend tells us the Ethiopians are treated "like niggers" but when I ask, to clarify, whether they are thought of as black (as opposed to white), another friend (of similar social position) insists that they are not black—they are "*shoko*" (chocolate). The conversation continues: we are told that yes, there is terrible racism against the Ethiopians, just like there is racism against the new Russian immigrants, and just like there is racism against homosexuals. The term *racism* is used without any intended correspondence to what might be called a "race."[5] Given this stretched usage of the word *racism,* which now seems to mean discrimination against any sort of group, it is still unclear what being white signifies in Israel. What is clear is that to focus on whiteness as of primary significance in determining where one stands with respect to racism here would be to (mis)apply a framework imported from elsewhere.

Ami: Following the same conversation you have already described, I feel the perhaps perverse need to reexamine what race/ethnicity may mean here now and begin to wonder about my last claim regarding the local situation. Namely, am I right to believe that the Jewish Israeli orientation toward Europe and North America just flavors but does not fully color the local ethnic/racial distinctions? There is obviously antiblack racism here and now that targets most harshly the non-Jewish African guest workers who have been deployed as replacement for the cheap labor force from Palestine (the West Bank and Gaza Strip). They are treated badly, particularly when here illegally, and are called *kushim,* literally meaning people from Kush, a biblical name for Africa. In local parlance, especially when used by children, *kushim* is meant to insult.[6] Still, the local form of antiblack racism is not the same as antiblack racism in the United States, which seems so totalizing because it colors one wholly black under the "one drop rule."[7] In light of U.S. understandings, the local form of antiblack racism is not too intelligible because what is perceived as one's biological Jewishness seems to affect one's color, acting perhaps as a "reverse one drop rule" that "lightens" one's color (as is clear from the case of the "*shoko*" Ethiopian Jews). This perceived biological Jewishness, and cultural Jewishness like that of the convert, may, however, act quite differently. Instead of functioning as a kind of a "reverse one drop rule," Jewishness may displace color as the primary and most significant marker of racial/ethnic distinctions recentering what still counts much more here, the nation, and therefore the Jewish/Arab binary.

There is something else, though, that needs to be taken into consideration, which is the possibility that while the Jewish/Arab binary is still primary here, Israel, like other countries in the global socioeconomic center and its immediate borders, is also experiencing the development of additional forms of racism.[8] Such a change may be facilitated by socioeconomic shifts including, locally, the introduction of guest workers who, though not Jewish and also not Arab, require different ways to be marked as unlike in a society where marking the other as other is an ingrained habit. This may explain, at least in part, why the term *racism* is used here so vaguely and seems to encompass any form of discrimination or bad attitude based on group membership. Thus, for example, secular Israeli Jews are accused of racism against the very Jewish orthodox, the *haredim*, who are both *Ashkenazi* and *Mizrachi* (meaning Eastern or Oriental and used interchangeably with *Spharadi*, a term that in the past was reserved to refer to Ladino-speaking Jews who traced their ancestry back to Spain and their legacy to the Spanish expulsion of Jews in 1492). In part, though, the extended domain of the term *racism* may be simply the result of the fact that from the beginning it was used without much precision. The term was borrowed in the late 1960s from U.S. discourses by local activists organizing themselves in protest of discrimination against *Mizrachi* Jews along U.S. models and even naming themselves the Black Panthers. Prior to that, the discrimination against *Mizrachi* Jews was discussed with reference to ethnicity but not to the idea of race, as was the discrimination against Arabs. The spread of support for antidiscrimination demands seems to have brought with it a popularization and very elastic use of the term *racism*.

But why am I talking about racism, even the local kind, when what I wanted to do when I started to describe whiteness as not very significant in the Israeli fabric of social meanings was to begin to explain my confusion about whiteness as a category, even after so many years in the United States? This confusion began when I had to fill out the first U.S. form that asked me what my race was. It was a confusion that I could not resolve

with the answer given to me when I requested help: that since I was by na-
tionality Israeli, hence, from the Middle East, I was Caucasian or white.

Having a formula to rely on when asked by a form about my race
is not the same as knowing that I have a race, an idea that my education
implied was at best bizarre, as well as terribly dangerous, as should have
been rather clear from World War II and the Nazi Judeocide. Moreover,
were I to have a race, the one I was supposed to have by virtue of *my*
history was not included on the form; I was Jewish and not white or
Caucasian.

Lisa: I have been apprehensive about light-skinned, generally *Ashkenazi* Jews in the United States who claim to not quite be white, including
immigrants such as you who report that although they know they are considered white in the United States, such a classification feels imposed and
foreign and not a right fit. In the context of discussions of U.S. racism, such
claims have seemed both irrelevant and evasive of responsibility for white
racism.[9] When I first heard you claim that it still felt strange to you to be
labeled "white," I could not really believe that your reluctance to accept
the designation could have its source in something other than evasion. I
could not imagine this other source because I could not fully conceive of
the black/white binary as decentered and therefore could not see how the
importance of being white—and the responsibility for acknowledging
oneself as white—could be diminished. Now, from here in the Middle
East, I can finally understand how "whiteness" can be of less than primary
importance; while not completely absent, whiteness conceived as a racial
marker is far from central. From within the shifted perspective that I have
even as a visitor here, my reflections on myself as someone who has learned
to think of myself as white reveal a strangeness.

Here in Israel, it seems that nobody actually learns to *be* white—to
experience themselves as white—in any very meaningful sense. Coming
from here to the United States, a Jewish Israeli would "become" white in
one magical moment of encountering the Immigration and Naturalization
Service but would have missed out on all the training that makes it seem
natural to be white, all the training in which a self-concept as white becomes inseparable from one's experience of the rest of the world. The moment is magical in that it signifies a becoming-white that takes place all at
once; it is an official granting of whiteness where before there was none.
It is a promise, too, that one will be treated as white every day in the new
country—a promise made, though, to someone who has not yet come to
know firsthand its importance. But the whiteness that is granted magically

like this is not the same whiteness that has become internal to those of us who grew up with it.

I want to get at the difference between these two kinds of whiteness because my sense is that one cannot reduce being white to having white privilege. To do so is to fail to notice the difference between learning to experience oneself as white, with whiteness as fundamental to one's self (as in my case), and missing out on that learning, yet appearing externally indistinguishable from someone who has done the learning (as in your case). It is true that (light-skinned, generally *Ashkenazi*) Jews, whether immigrant or raised in an unassimilated way in the United States, are largely taken to be white, both in official contexts and in everyday "commonsense" ways (on the street, on the job market, in social situations),[10] and they are accorded what can be called white privilege, especially when the right class factors figure in. Nonetheless, there is something distinct and additional about experiencing oneself as white. It seems that certain things, such as being an immigrant from a country without a racial state (or with a different one), or being raised as clearly an ethnic outsider within the United States (such as Jews can be if they are not assimilated, especially in those parts of the United States where "white," "Christian," and "American" function inseparably), can create a void in which one *is* not fully white though one is treated as white.

What, then, does one learn when one learns to *be* white in the United States? What did I learn (being assimilated enough) that makes me fully white, that you never got to learn, and that makes you less than fully fitted into whiteness (i.e., not "properly" socialized)? To be fully white is to have the habits of whiteness, habits that most whites in the United States probably begin practicing in childhood and that seem to involve learning how to distinguish oneself from specific others, especially blacks, and to distinguish as one distinguishes the superior from the inferior, the norm from the aberration, the trustworthy from the scary, the valuable from the dispensable. Perhaps these early-learned habits are among the things that an adult immigrant can never really attain, even after substantial assimilation. I have often noticed that you do not catch my references to the details of a U.S. childhood—such things as nursery rhymes and taunts and children's books and games, or standing in grade-school classrooms where one is expected to recite "I pledge allegiance to the flag of the United States of America . . ."—and even if I tell you about them they will not be a part of you as they are a part of me, for they will not make you smile or cringe with memories; you may

read *Goodnight Moon* aloud now to a friend's child, but it will reverber-
ate with nothing from your past; you may be called upon to salute the
American flag—and refuse—but it brings forth no memories, as it does
for me, of refusing to do so as a child. And so it dawned on me that
along with missing out on early affective training in such things, you
were not trained at a young age in how to experience yourself as white.
Whatever you have learned about being white as an adult has no childhood or adolescent reference point. Without this, there must be no un-
dercurrent feeling of loss in struggling to rid oneself of the sense of superiority that comes with a white identity.

My sense of whiteness always has a childhood or adolescent reference
point. My sense of myself as white is inseparable from my sense of myself
as being from Newton, Massachusetts, a town that blacks could enter only
as outsiders. It was certainly as outsiders that the METCO kids—black students bussed in from Boston—came to the Newton public schools; we
(white, middle- and upper-middle-class youth, self-confident in our belonging in the town and the schools) never called them black, referring to
them only as "the METCO kids." And though we were liberal and therefore thought of ourselves as very, very different from those racist white
people who had thrown stones at the buses, and though we were quite
cognizant of and sometimes active against the racist practice of tracking
"the METCO kids" into the lowest-level classes, the messages about who
we were as whites had sunk in. Despite the euphemistic terms we used to
mask it, we knew ourselves as white in relation to our opposite, black. My
image of "us" (here many whites get excluded from my "we" because
"they" were not the right class; nevertheless, my deepest sense of being
white is indeed this elite one, undoubtedly a different sense of whiteness
than those with different class backgrounds have) was that we were smart,
sometimes so smart that others would resent it and tease us; we did not get
pregnant and drop out; we did drugs, but the fun, recreational kind, not the
kind that one must be desperate to go near; we had professional parents at
home; we were profound thinkers and read the best literature; we were not
loud and did not take up the whole hallway at school by walking in a tight
throng; the best of us did not even watch television. While there were
many divisions among groups of kids when I was growing up, based on
class, ethnicity, and just plain popularity, they were not *all* unbridgeable.
However, one was absolutely unbridgeable: I knew of not one single
friendship between any of us white students and any of "the METCO
kids."

Once when I was in college, a midwestern liberal arts college where friendships between blacks and whites were at least possible, I met a black student who introduced himself as being from Roxbury, one of the parts of Boston from which "the METCO kids" were bussed to suburbs including Newton. Suddenly the weight of having a childhood reference point for race bore down on me. There I was in college, raised consciousness and all, in the middle of the passionate if misguided process of trying to jump out of my white skin to avoid being one of the bad guys in the racist schema of things. I knew that if I said at that moment where I was from, my whiteness in the face of his blackness would be overwhelming, inescapable, and somehow terribly wrong. It was not that *any* whiteness and *any* blackness could have had this effect. It was that the whiteness that I was, that I had learned early on, was meant to be superior to the blackness that he was. It seemed that there could be, for me, no undoing of that sense of superiority—felt now by me as racist and shameful—as long as I was thrown back by what presented themselves as simple facts: I was from Newton; he was from Roxbury.

What would it be like to be suddenly designated white and yet have none of this early, weighty socialization in what it means to be white?

Ami: To me the designation "white" has yet to seem fitting in just the right way because it feels so shallow, especially in comparison to my designation as a Jewish Israeli. I am not certain how to describe the difference of feeling one as "shallow" and the other as "deep" except by pointing out that when "hailed" as white, I am still surprised and have to tell myself that yes it is me who is "hailed." I experience a similar surprise only when I am not "hailed" as Jewish Israeli, which now happens sometimes during the first days back in Israel, when my Hebrew is still American English accented. But resisting the designation of "white," which I did for a while after arriving in the United States, eventually put me in an ethicopolitically peculiar place. I understood the antiracist struggle in the United States, and especially the feminist one (being so identity based), as requiring that I identify publicly as white to be seen as a credible ally. Nonetheless, as my experience of the failure of "hailing" suggests, this identification is quite formulaic: I identify publicly as a being that falls under a social category, but I do not have much of a sense of myself as a being that falls under that category, perhaps because this sense is a function of the play of complex micro and macro social forces, many of which, as you point out, shape one's feel of self during early socialization.

What has been less formulaic for me is learning that I am a being who is most usually accorded a measure of white privilege in the United States and who is therefore granted certain courtesies, deferences, opportunities, and safeties. Because I have grown up as a Jewish Israeli, I have also been socialized into a variety of privileges that are part of the Israeli scene, with its ethnic hierarchies.[11] Thus, for example, I was quite used to being treated in a friendly enough fashion by salespersons, unlike Jews from North Africa, and to not being suspected by the police when taking a walk through the neighborhood no matter how late at night, which no Palestinian in Israel can take for granted when not in Jewish Israeli company.

While these examples may seem quite innocuous, they are about suspicion, and suspicion of Palestinians as harboring danger to Jews undergirds elaborate surveillance routines in the Israeli situation, many of which are performed by every Jewish Israeli citizen automatically. Like all other Jewish Israelis, I have been mobilized by the state since I was very young and taught to "recognize" Arabs (we did not "recognize" Palestinians because we denied their national identity), to use almost imperceptible kinds of difference to succeed in performing these acts of "recognition," and always to be alert to the possibility of their "passing." Though burdened with vigilance, as long as I embodied the gestures, posture, modes of talking and modes of dress of the *Sabra*, I was free from suspicion by others. This freedom, requiring as it does the fashioning of the body in distinction from other bodies, is a Jewish Israeli privilege that makes some white privileges familiar.

Being accorded white privilege, especially when social privilege is familiar, may tempt immigrants who do not come from countries in which whiteness is a particularly significant marker of identity to begin to develop a sense of ourselves as white and hence to refashion ourselves into people with white identities. This temptation is hard to resist because some level of assimilation, or of hybridization, is simply necessary for survival in one's new country. Our transformations into white-identified people may, however, come about much less consciously, since being designated white may slowly interpolate us into whiteness. White privilege is accorded as part of a practice, and practice subjectifies through habituation. So, while being white is different from merely being designated white, one may become used to whiteness precisely because one is designated and treated as if one is white.

I do not think, though, that because one can be and is interpolated into whiteness through practices that accord one white privilege, one becomes the same kind of white as one who has been socialized to be white from early on. What one will continue to lack are the multiple ways in which early socialization gives one's racialized self a sense of depth. While in the context of U.S. antiracist struggle it does not seem to be such a bad thing to lack depth in one's sense of whiteness, for an immigrant, the lack is a reminder of her or his foreignness, of something about her or him that is forever inassimilable. One can choose to celebrate this, and yet one must recognize that there is always something psychologically costly to *being* "other."

ENDNOTES

1. A recent radio poll has shown that the new immigrants from Russia are resented by more than 50 percent of the established Jewish Israeli population. Among the things believed by respondents is that they compete with Jewish Israelis for work, they cheapen labor, and their professional degrees are a sham. Thirty-four percent of the respondents even found the new Russian immigrants frightening. See the July 10, 1997, summary of findings in the *Jerusalem Post*, p. 4.
2. See Ella Shohat, "Spharadim in Israel: Zionism from the Standpoint of Its Jewish Victims," *Social Text* 7, nos. 1–2 (Fall 1988): 1–36.
3. I borrow this terminology from Michael Omi and Howard Winant, *Racial Formation in the United States: From the 1960s to the 1990s* (New York: Routledge, 1994).
4. According to the definitions used by the U.S. federal government, one is "WHITE (Not of Hispanic Origin)" if one is "a person having origins in any of the original peoples of Europe, North Africa, or the Middle East."
5. For instance, the National Union of Students, in their antiracism campaign, focuses on eliminating the use of what it refers to as "racist" slogans such as "Dirty Ethiopian," "Maniac Ashkenazi," "Slippery Moroccan," and "Russian Whore" and, after being criticized by Arab students for a glaring omission, claims to have also intended targeting the slogan "A Good Arab Is a Dead Arab." See "City Lights," supplement to the *Jerusalem Post* 5, no. 179 (July 11, 1997): 2.
6. There have been several newspaper reports about this. See, for example, a series of articles about the new Tel Aviveans in *Ha'ir*, June and July 1997.
7. See Ian F. Haney Lopez, *White by Law: The Legal Construction of Race* (New York: New York University Press, 1996). At the same time, though, the "one drop rule" is under attack by the "mixed race" movement. While its politics needs examining (see Lisa Tessman, "The Racial Politics of Mixed-Race," *Journal of Social*

Philosophy 30, no. 2 (Fall 1999), the fact of its organization and its growing success, together with the organization and success of other ethnic/racial groups in the United States, may indicate a change of the racial/ethnic formation of the United States.

8. Zigmunt Bauman calls attention to changes of this kind in Europe in his discussion of anti-Semitism in *Life in Fragments: Essays in Postmodern Morality* (Oxford: Blackwell, 1995), 206–22. See also Etienne Balibar's "Is There a Neo-Racism?" in *Race, Nation, Class: Ambiguous Identities*, ed. Etienne Balibar and Immanuel Wallerstein (Paris: Editions La Découverte, 1988; London: Verso, 1991), 17–28.

9. See, for instance, Gloria Anzaldúa's complaints about those whom she calls "white Jewishwomen" (which she distinguishes from "Jewish women-of-color"), who, in a class she taught about women of color, "did not want to identify as white." She writes, "Some declared they felt they 'belonged' more to the women-of-color group than they did to the white group. Because they felt isolated and excluded, they felt that their oppressions were the same or similar to those of women-of-color." "Haciendo Caras, una Entrada" in *Making Face, Making Soul/Haciendo Caras: Creative and Critical Perspectives by Women of Color*, ed. Gloria Anzaldúa (San Francisco: Aunt Lute, 1990), xx. Anzaldúa saw this as a failure to be accountable for white racism. A very nuanced consideration of whether and how Jews are white in the United States (an account that in fact quelled some of my apprehension) can be found in Melanie Kaye/Kantrowitz, "Jews, Class, Color, and the Cost of Whiteness," in *The Issue is Power* (San Francisco: Aunt Lute, 1992), and "Jews in the U.S.: The Rising Costs of Whiteness," in *Names We Call Home: Autobiography on Racial Identity*, ed. Becky Thompson and Sangeeta Tyagi (New York: Routledge, 1996).

10. Some dark-skinned Jews may be in an especially interesting position of being officially classified as white yet not counting as white in "commonsense" ways.

11. In her "White Privilege: Unpacking the Invisible Knapsack," *Peace and Freedom* (July/August 1989): 10–12, Peggy McIntosh lists twenty-six items that exemplify white privilege in the United States. The list can work with appropriate adjustments when thinking through Jewish Israeli privilege relative to Palestinian Israeli, *Ashkenazi* privilege relative to *Mizrachi,* as well as about aspects of class privilege.

Epilogue

Hey, don't be fooled. Where we live philosophy is white white white. White men, white marble, white hair, white shirts under blue blazers and red ties. Hey, did you know that the American translation of the ancient Greek word Sophia *is* "WHITE"? *Filia* + *Sophia* = *Friend to Whiteness Everywhere. Now, there are a number of Black men who teach and write philosophy in the U.S. of A., suitably scaring those who cling to the whiteness of wisdom. Don't get me wrong—that's a good thing. But where is the philosophical posse of black and brown women? Sometimes I think that's what it would take to turn things around. . . .*

Related Reading

Alexander, M. Jacqui, and Chandra Talapade Mohanty, eds. 1997. *Feminist Genealogies, Colonial Legacies, Democratic Futures*. New York: Routledge.

Allen, Paula Gunn. 1986. *The Sacred Hoop: Recovering the Feminine in American Indian Traditions*. Boston: Beacon.

Allen, Theodore W. *The Invention of the White Race*. London: Verso.

Allison, Dorothy. 1989. *Trash*. Ithaca, N.Y.: Firebrand.

————. 1992. *Bastard out of Carolina*. New York: Plume.

————. 1994. *Skin: Talking about Sex, Class and Literature*. Ithaca, N.Y.: Firebrand.

————. 1995. *Two or Three Things I Know for Sure*. New York: Dutton.

Amin, Samir. 1989. *Eurocentrism*. London: Zed.

Anderson, Benedict. 1983. *Imagined Communities: Reflections on the Origins and Spread of Nationalism*. London: Verso.

Anzaldúa, Gloria. 1987. *Borderlands/La Frontera: The New Mestiza*. San Francisco: Aunt Lute.

————, ed. 1990. *Making Face, Making Soul/Haciendo Caras: Creative and Critical Perspectives by Women of Color*. San Francisco: Aunt Lute.

Appiah, Kwame Anthony. 1992. *In My Father's House: Africa in the Philosophy of Culture*. New York: Oxford University Press.

Appiah, Kwame Anthony, and Henry Louis Gates, Jr., eds. 1998. *Transition* 7, no. 1, The White Issue.

Aptheker, Bettina. 1982. *Women's Legacy: Essays on Race, Sex, and Class*. Amherst: University of Massachusetts Press.

————. 1989. *Tapestries of Life: Women's Work, Women's Consciousness and the Meaning of Daily Experience*. Amherst: University of Massachusetts Press.

Asante, Molefi Kete. 1987. *The Afrocentric Idea*. Philadelphia: Temple University Press.

Balibar, Etienne, and Immanuel Wallerstein. 1991. *Race, Nation, Class: Ambiguous Identities*. London: Verso.

Beaver, Patricia, and Carol Hill, eds. 1998. *Cultural Diversity in the U.S. South: Anthropological Contributions to a Region in Change*. Athens: University of Georgia Press.

Beck, Evelyn Torton, ed. 1982. *Nice Jewish Girls: A Lesbian Anthology.* Watertown, Mass.: Persephone.

Behar, Ruth. 1994. *Translated Woman: Crossing the Border with Esperanza's Story.* Boston: Beacon.

Behar, Ruth, and Deborah Gordon, eds. 1996. *Women Writing Culture.* Berkeley: University of California Press.

———. 1997. *The Vulnerable Observer: Anthropology That Breaks Your Heart.* Boston: Beacon.

Bethel, Lorraine. 1979. "What Chou Mean We, White Girl?" *Conditions Five: The Black Woman's Issue,* no. 2, ed. Lorraine Bethel and Barbara Smith.

Bowser, Benjamin P., ed. 1995. *Racism and Anti-Racism in World Perspective.* London: Sage.

Blee, Kathleen. 1991. *Women of the Klan: Racism and Gender in the 1920s.* Berkeley: University of California Press.

Blunt, Alison. 1994. *Travel, Gender, and Imperialism: Mary Kingsley and West Africa.* New York: Guilford.

Bulkin, Elly, Minnie Bruce Pratt, and Barbara Smith. 1984. *Yours in Struggle: Three Feminist Perspectives on Anti-Semitism and Racism.* Ithaca, N.Y.: Firebrand.

Bullard, Robert, ed. 1993. *Confronting Environmental Racism: Voices from the Grassroots.* Boston: South End.

Caraway, Nancie. 1991. *Segregated Sisterhood: Racism and the Politics of American Feminism.* Knoxville: University of Tennessee Press.

Castillo, Debra. 1992. *Talking Back: Toward a Latin American Feminist Literary Criticism.* Ithaca, N.Y.: Cornell University Press.

Center for Democratic Renewal. 1987. *They Don't All Wear Sheets: A Chronology of Racist and Far Right Violence, 1980–1986.* Atlanta: Center for Democratic Renewal.

———. 1994. *A Year of Intolerance: A Review of Hate Group Activities and Ideologies in 1994.* Atlanta: Center for Democratic Renewal.

———. 1995. *Paramilitary Right Moves Center Stage: Overview of Militias, Hate Groups, and Intolerance in 1995.* Atlanta: Center for Democratic Renewal.

Center for Contemporary Cultural Studies. 1982. *The Empire Strikes Back: Race and Racism in 70s Britain.* London: Hutchinson.

Cesaire, Aime. 1972. *Discourse on Colonialism.* New York: Monthly Review Press.

Chapkis, Wendy. 1986. *Beauty Secrets: Women and the Politics of Appearance.* Boston: South End.

Chaudhuri, Nupur, and Margaret Strobel. 1992. *Western Women and Imperialism: Complicity and Resistance.* Bloomington: Indiana University Press.

Christian, Barbara. 1986. *Black Feminist Criticism.* New York: Pergamon.

Chrystos. 1988. *Not Vanishing.* Vancouver: Press Gang.

————. 1991. *Dream On.* Vancouver: Press Gang.

Collins, Patricia Hill. 1990. *Black Feminist Thought: Knowledge, Consciousness, and the Politics of Empowerment.* New York: Routledge.

————. 1998. *Fighting Words: Black Women and the Search for Justice.* Minneapolis: University of Minnesota Press.

Combahee River Collective. 1983. "The Combahee River Collective Statement." In *Home Girls: A Black Feminist Anthology,* ed. Barbara Smith. New York: Kitchen Table: Women of Color Press.

Dash, Julie, and bell hooks. 1992. *Daughters of the Dust: The Making of an African American Woman's Film.* New York: New Press.

DuBois, W. E. B. 1989. *The Souls of Black Folk.* New York: Penguin.

Davis, Angela Y. 1981. *Women, Race, and Class.* New York: Random House.

————. 1984. *Women, Culture, and Politics.* New York: Random House.

Delgado, Richard, ed. 1995. *Critical Race Theory: The Cutting Edge.* Philadelphia: Temple University Press.

Delgado, Richard, and Jean Stefancic, eds. 1997. *Critical White Studies: Looking Behind the Mirror.* Philadelphia: Temple University Press.

Dominguez, Virginia. 1986. *White by Definition: Social Classification in Creole Louisiana.* New Brunswick, N.J.: Rutgers University Press.

Donald, James, and Ali Rattansi, eds. 1992. *Race, Culture, and Difference.* London: Sage.

Essed, Philomena. 1990. *Everyday Racism: Reports from Women of Two Cultures.* Claremont, Calif.: Hunter House.

Ezorsky, Gertrude. 1991. *Racism and Justice: The Case for Affirmative Action.* Ithaca, N.Y.: Cornell University Press.

Fanon, Franz. 1963. *The Wretched of the Earth.* New York: Grove.

————. 1967. *Black Skin, White Masks.* New York: Grove.

Fine, Michelle, Lois Weis, Linda C. Powell, and L. Mun Wang, eds. 1997. *Off White: Readings on Race, Power, and Society.* New York: Routledge.

Frankenberg, Ruth. 1993. *White Women, Race Matters: The Social Construction of Whiteness.* Minneapolis: University of Minnesota Press.

————. 1997. *Displacing Whiteness: Essays in Social and Cultural Criticism.* Durham, N.C.: Duke University Press.

Fusco, Coco. 1995. *English Is Broken Here: Notes on Cultural Fusion in the Americas.* New York: New Press.

————, ed. 1997. *Displacing Whiteness: Essays in Social and Cultural Criticism.* Durham, N.C.: Duke University Press.

Frye, Marilyn. 1983. *The Politics of Reality: Essays in Feminist Theory.* Freedom, Calif.: Crossing.

————. 1992. *The Willful Virgin: Essays in Feminism.* Freedom, Calif.: Crossing.

Gates, Henry Louis, Jr. 1985. "Race." In *Writing and Difference.* Chicago: University of Chicago Press.

Genovese, Elizabeth Fox. 1988. *Within the Plantation Household: Black and White Women of the Old South.* Chapel Hill: University of North Carolina Press.

Gilroy, Paul. 1987. *There Ain't No Black in the Union Jack.* London: Hutchinson.

————. 1993. *The Black Atlantic: Modernity and Double Consciousness.* Cambridge, Mass.: Harvard University Press.

————. 1993. *Small Acts: Thoughts on the Politics of Black Cultures.* London: Serpent's Tail.

Goldberg, David Theo, ed. *The Anatomy of Racism.* Minneapolis: University of Minnesota Press.

————. 1993. *Racist Culture: Philosophy and the Politics of Meaning.* Cambridge: Blackwell.

————. 1994. *Multiculturalism: A Critical Reader.* Oxford: Blackwell.

Gonzalez, Ray. 1992. *Without Discovery: A Native Response to Columbus.* Seattle: Broken Moon.

Gooding-Williams, Robert, ed. 1993. *Reading Rodney King, Reading Urban Uprising.* New York: Routledge.

Gordon, Lewis. 1997. *Her Majesty's Other Children: Sketches of Racism from a Neocolonial Age.* Lanham, Md.: Rowman & Littlefield.

Grewd, Inderpal, and Caren Kaplan, eds. 1994. *Scattered Hegemonies: Postmodernity and Transnational Feminist Practice.* Minneapolis: University of Minnesota Press.

Gurganus, Allan. 1990. *White People.* New York: Ivy.

Grossberg, Lawrence, Cary Nelson, and Paula Treichler, eds. 1992. *Cultural Studies.* New York: Routledge.

Gwaltney, John Langston. 1980. *Drylongso: A Self Portrait of Black America*. New York: Random House.

Hall, Catherine. 1992. *White, Male, and Middle Class*. Cambridge: Polity.

Hall, Kim. 1990. "Learning to Touch Honestly: A White Lesbian's Struggle with Racism." In *Lesbian Philosophies and Cultures*, ed. Jeffner Allen. Albany: State University of New York Press.

Hansberry, Lorraine. 1969. *To Be Young, Gifted, and Black*. Englewood Cliffs, N.J.: Random House.

Harding, Sandra, ed. 1993. *The "Racial" Economy of Science: Toward a Democratic Future*. Bloomington: Indiana University Press.

———. 1998. *Is Science Multicultural? Postcolonialisms, Feminisms, and Epistemologies*. Bloomington: Indiana University Press.

hooks, bell. 1981. *Ain't I a Woman: Black Women and Feminism*. Boston: South End.

———. 1984. *Feminist Theory from Margin to Center*. Boston: South End.

———. 1989. *Talking Back: Thinking Feminist, Thinking Black*. Boston: South End.

———. 1990. *Yearning: Race, Gender, and Cultural Politics*. Boston: South End.

———. 1992. *Black Looks: Race and Representation*. Boston: South End.

———. 1995. *Killing Rage: Ending Racism*. New York: Holt.

———. 1996. *Bone Black: Memories of Girlhood*. New York: Holt.

Horsman, Reginald. 1981. *Race and Manifest Destiny: The Origins of American Racial Anglo-Saxonism*. Cambridge, Mass.: Harvard University Press.

Huckfeldt, Robert, and Carole Weitzel Kohfeld. 1989. *Race and the Decline of Class in American Politics*. Urbana: University of Illinois Press.

Hull, Gloria T., Patricia B. Scott, and Barbara Smith, eds. 1982. *All the Women Are White, All the Blacks Are Men, But Some of Us Are Brave: Black Women's Studies*. New York: Feminist.

Hulme, Peter. 1986. *Colonial Encounters: Europe and the Native Caribbean, 1492–1797*. London: Methuen.

Hulme, Peter, and Neil Whitehead. 1992. *Wild Majesty: Encounters with Caribs from Columbus to the Present Day*. Oxford: Oxford University Press.

Ignatiev, Noel. 1995. *How the Irish Became White*. New York: Routledge.

Jones, Simon. 1988. *Black Culture, White Youth: The Reggae Culture from JA to UK*. London: Macmillan.

Jordan, June. 1992. *Technical Difficulties: Selected Political Essays*. London: Virago.

Joseph, Gloria, and Jill Lewis. 1981. *Common Differences: Conflicts in Black and White Feminist Perspectives.* Boston: South End.

Kaye/Kantrowitz, Melanie, and Irena Klepfisz, eds. 1989. *The Tribe of Dina: A Jewish Women's Anthology.* Boston: Beacon.

King, Katie. 1994. *Theory in Its Feminist Travels: Conversations in U.S. Women's Movements.* Bloomington: Indiana University Press.

Kingston, Maxine Hong. 1976. *The Woman Warrior.* New York: Vintage.

Klepfisz, Irena. 1990. *Dreams of an Insomniac: Jewish Feminist Essays, Speeches, and Diatribes.* Portland: Eighth Mountain Press.

Lerner, Gerda. 1973. *Black Women in White America: A Documentary History.* New York: Random House.

Lopez, Ian Haney. 1996. *White by Law.* New York: New York University Press.

Lorde, Audre. 1992. *Undersong: Chosen Poems Old and New.* New York: Norton.

———. 1986. *Our Dead behind Us.* New York: Norton.

———. 1984. *Sister Outsider.* Freedom, Calif.: Crossing.

Lugones, María. 1998. "El Pasar Discontinuo do la Cachapera/Tortilera del Barrio a la Barra al Movimiento/The Discontinuous Passing of the Cachapera/Tortillera from the Barrio to the Bar to the Movement." In *Daring to be Good: Essays in Feminist Ethico-Politics,* ed. Bat-Ami Bar On and Ann Ferguson. New York: Routledge.

———. 1994. "Purity, Impurity, and Separation." *Signs* 19, no. 2: 458–79.

———. 1991. "On the Logic of Pluralist Feminism." In *Feminist Ethics,* ed. Claudia Card. Lawrence: University of Kansas Press.

———. 1987. "Playfulness, 'World'-Travelling, and Loving Perception." *Hypatia* 2, no. 2: 3–19.

Lugones, María, and Elizabeth Spelman. 1990. "Have We Got a Theory for You! Cultural Imperialism and the Demand for the Woman's Voice." In *Hypatia Reborn: Essays in Feminist Philosophy,* ed. Asisah al-Hibri and Margaret A. Simons. Bloomington: Indiana University Press.

Martin, Biddy, and Chandra Talpade Mohanty. 1986. "Feminist Politics: What's Home Got to Do with It." In *Feminist Studies/Critical Studies,* ed. Teresa De Lauretis. Bloomington: Indiana University Press.

McKinley, Catherine E., and L. Joyce DeLaney, eds. 1995. *Afrekete: An Anthology of Black Lesbian Writing.* New York: Doubleday.

Matsuda, Mari J., Charles R. Lawrence III, Richard Delgado, and Kimberle Williams Crenshaw. 1993. *Words That Wound: Critical Race Theory, Assaultive Speech, and the First Amendment.* Boulder, Colo.: Westview.

Memmi, Albert. 1967. *The Colonizer and the Colonized.* Boston: Beacon.

Mills, Charles. 1997. *The Racial Contract.* Ithaca, N.Y. : Cornell University Press, 1997.

Minh-Ha, Trinh T. 1989. *Woman, Native, Other: Writing Postcoloniality and Feminism.* Bloomington: Indiana University Press.

————. 1991. *When the Moon Waxes Red: Representation, Gender and Cultural Politics.* London: Routledge.

Mohanty, Chandra Talpade, Ann Russo, and Lourdes Torres, eds. 1991. *Third World Women and the Politics of Feminism.* Bloomington: Indiana University Press.

Moraga, Cherrie. 1983. *Loving in the War Years: Lo Que Nunca Pasa por Sus Labios.* Boston: South End.

Morrison, Toni. 1992. *Playing in the Dark: Whiteness and the Literary Imagination.* Cambridge, Mass.: Harvard University Press.

Mudimbe, V. Y. 1988. *The Invention of Africa.* Bloomington: Indiana University Press.

Naples, Nancy A. 1998. *Community Activism and Feminist Politics: Organizing Across Race, Class, and Gender.* New York: Routledge.

Nederveen Pieterse, J. P. 1992. *White on Black: Images of Africa and Blacks in Western Popular Culture.* London: Yale University Press.

Ngugi wa Thiong'o. 1986. *Decolonising the Mind: The Politics of Language in African Literature.* London: Currey.

Oliver, Melvin L., and Thomas M. Shapiro. 1995. *Black Welath/White Wealth: A New Perspective on Racial Inequality.* New York: Routledge.

Omi, Michael, and Howard Winant. 1986. *Racial Formation in the United States: From the 1960s to the 1980s.* New York: Routledge.

Outlaw, Lucius T. 1996. *On Race and Philosophy.* New York and London: Routledge.

Poliakov, Leon. 1974. *The Aryan Myth: A History of Racist and Nationalist Ideas in Europe.* London: Weidenfeld & Nicholson.

Pratt, Mary Louise. 1992. *Imperial Eyes: Travel Writing and Transculturation.* London: Routledge.

Pratt, Minnie Bruce, Barbara Smith, and Elly Bulkin, eds. 1984. *Yours in Struggle: Three Feminist Perspectives on Anti-Semitism and Racism.* Ithaca, N.Y.: Firebrand.

Ratti, Rakesh, ed. 1993. *A Lotus of Another Color: An Unfolding of the South Asian Gay and Lesbian Experience.* Boston: Alyson Publications.

Rich, Adrienne. 1979. *On Lies, Secrets, and Silence: Selected Prose 1966–1978.* New York: Norton.

————. 1981. *A Wild Patience Has Taken Me This Far: Poems 1978–1981.* New York: Norton.

Roediger, David R. 1990. *The Wages of Whiteness: Race and the Making of the American Working Class.* New York: Verso.

————. 1994. *Towards the Abolition of Whiteness: Essays on Race, Politics, and Working Class History.* London: Verso.

Root, Maria. 1996. *Racially Mixed People in America.* Knobbier Park, Calif.: Sage.

Rosaldo, Renato. 1988. *Culture and Truth: The Remaking of Social Analysis.* Boston: Beacon.

Said, Edward. 1978. *Orientalism.* London: Routledge & Kegan Paul.

————. 1985. *After the Last Sky: Palestinian Lives.* New York: Pantheon.

————. 1993. *Culture and Imperialism.* London: Chatto & Windus.

Scales-Trent, Judy. 1995. *Notes of a White Black Woman.* University Park: Pennsylvania State University Press.

Segrest, Mab. 1986. *My Mama's Dead Squirrel: Lesbian Essays on Southern Culture.* Ithaca, N.Y.: Firebrand.

————. 1994. *Memoir of a Race Traitor.* Boston: South End.

Shohat, Ella, and Robert Stam. 1994. *Unthinking Eurocentrism: Multiculturalism and the Media.* New York and London: Routledge.

Silko, Leslie Marmon. 1997. *Yellow Woman and a Beauty of the Spirit.* New York: Simon & Schuster.

Smith, Barbara, ed. 1983. *Home Girls: A Black Feminist Anthology.* New York: Kitchen Table: Women of Color Press.

Spelman, Elizabeth V. 1988. *Inessential Woman: Problems of Exclusion in Feminist Thought.* Boston: Beacon.

Spivak, Gayatri Chakravorty. 1987. *In Other Worlds: Essays in Cultural Politics.* London: Methuen.

————. 1990. *The Post-Colonial Critic: Interviews, Strategies, Dialogues,* ed. Sarah Harasym. New York: Routledge.

Stuckey, Sterling. 1987. *Slave Culture: Nationalist Theory and the Foundations of Black America.* New York: Oxford University Press.

Thompson, Becky, and Sangeeta Tyagi, eds. 1996. *Names We Call Home: Autobiography on Racial Identity.* New York: Routledge.

Walker, Alice. 1982. *The Color Purple.* New York: Pocket.

————. 1984. *In Search of Our Mothers' Gardens.* San Diego, Calif.: Harcourt Brace Jovanovich.

Walker, Alice, and Pratibha Parmar. 1996. *Warrior Marks: Female Genital Mutilation and the Sexual Blinding of Women.* San Diego, Calif.: Harcourt Brace.

Ware, Vron. 1992. *Beyond the Pale: White Women, Racism, and History.* London: Verso.

Washington, Mary Helen. 1988. *Invented Lives: Narratives of Black Women, 1860–1960.* New York: Doubleday.

West, Cornel. 1994. *Race Matters.* New York: Vintage.

Williams, Patricia J. 1991. *The Alchemy of Race and Rights: Diary of a Law Professor.* Cambridge, Mass.: Harvard University Press.

Williams, Patrick, and Laura Chrisman, eds. 1994. *Colonial Discourse and Post-Colonial Theory: A Reader.* New York: Columbia University Press.

Wray, Matt, and Annalee Newitz, eds. 1997. *White Trash: Race and Class in America.* New York: Routledge.

Young, Robert. 1990. *White Mythologies: Writing History and the West.* London: Routledge.

Zack, Naomi, ed. 1995. *American Mixed Race: The Culture of Microdiversity.* Lanham, Md.: Rowman & Littlefield.

Index

About the Contributors

ALISON BAILEY teaches philosophy and women's studies at Illinois State University. She is the author of *Posterity and Strategic Policy: A Moral Assessment of U.S. Strategic Weapons Options* (Lanham, Md.: University Press of America, 1989). Her essays have been published in *Hypatia, The Journal of Social Philosophy*, and *Philosophical Perspectives on Power and Domination*. Her current research interests focus on issues of shared moral responsibility in general and specifically on questions of how constructions of moral agency and responsibility are affected by race privilege. (baileya@ilstu.edu)

BAT-AMI BAR ON teaches philosophy and women's studies at the State University of New York at Binghamton. Her primary theoretical and activist interests are in violence, though she escapes them (often?) by pursuing other themes. She is the editor of *Daring to Be Good: Essays in Feminist Ethico-Politics*, with Ann Ferguson (New York: Routledge, 1998), *Women and Violence*, a special issue of *Hypatia* (Fall 1996), *Engendering Origins: Critical Feminist Readings of Plato and Aristotle*, and *Modern Engenderings: Critical Feminist Readings in the History of Modern Western Philosophy* (New York: SUNY Press, 1994).

CHRIS J. CUOMO is associate professor of philosophy and member of the women's studies program at the University of Cincinnati. She is the author of *Feminism and Ecological Communities: An Ethic of Flourishing* (New York: Routledge, 1998) and various essays on ethics, gender, and sexuality.

AMY EDGINGTON works for the public library in Little Rock, Arkansas. She is an artist and a longtime board member of The Women's Project. Her poetry and essays have been published in many feminist, lesbian, and gay journals and anthologies.

LAURIE FULLER, as both a student and teacher of women's studies, has been interested in and concerned about the ways that notions of race, sexuality, class, and other identity markers circulate in a classroom focused on gender issues. She brings this attention to her work as an assistant professor and women's studies coordinator at Northeastern Illinois University in Chicago. In her spare time she is an avid reader of science fiction and mystery novels as well as a weekend bicyclist and sports fan.

KIM Q. HALL is assistant professor of philosophy at Appalachian State University. She is currently completing a book entitled *Writing with a Woman in Mind* in which she considers methods of feminist theorizing located at the intersections of gender, race, class, and sexuality.

LINDA LÓPEZ MCALISTER comes from Los Angeles but went to New York for her education in philosophy—Barnard, City College of New York, and Cornell—where she earned her Ph.D. She has been an actor, a philosophy professor, an academic administrator, and most recently chair of women's studies at the University of South Florida. These days she writes on history of women in philosophy and on film. She is currently working on three books: one on feminist films of the 1990s, an edited collection (with Joyce Berkman) of articles on Edith Stein, and a history of feminist philosophy in the United States since the 1970s. She was honored by the Society for Women in Philosophy as their Distinguished Woman Philosopher for 1998.

LINDA M. PIERCE graduated with a B.A. in English literature and women studies at Western Washington University in 1995. She obtained an M.A. in literature from Western Washington University in 1997, specializing in postcolonial and feminist criticisms, and is currently studying Filipina and Filipina American literatures at the University of Arizona.

LISA TESSMAN teaches philosophy at the State University of New York in Binghamton. Her work in feminist theory and critical race theory focuses on ethics in the context of communities involved in liberatory struggles; in particular, she is concerned with the usefulness of virtue ethics for these communities. She is currently coediting a collection with Bat-Ami Bar On, to be entitled *Jewish Locations: Traversing Racialized Landscapes*.

JUDY SCALES-TRENT formerly a civil rights lawyer, is currently professor of law at State University of New York at Buffalo School of Law. She has written extensively on the intersection of race and gender in law and is the author of *Notes of a White Black Woman: Race, Color, Community* (State College, Penn.: Penn State Press, 1995).

NAOMI ZACK is associate professor in the Department of Philosophy at the University at Albany. She is author of: *Race and Mixed Race* (Philadelphia: Temple University Press, 1993), *Bachelors of Science: Seventeenth-Century Identity, Then and Now* (Philadelphia: Temple University Press, 1996), and *Thinking about Race*, a textbook (Belmont, Calif.: Wadsworth, 1998.) She has edited *American Mixed Race: The Culture of Microdiversity* (Lanham, Md.: Roman & Littlefield, 1995) and *RACE/SEX: Their Sameness, Difference and Interplay* (New York: Routledge, 1997).